PITCHERS

OF PERFECTION

PITCHERS OF PERFECTION

The Cy Young Award Winners

JOHN MARINO

MetroBooks

MetroBooks

An Imprint of Friedman/Fairfax Publishers

© 1996 by Michael Friedman Publishing Group, Inc.

Library of Congress Cataloging-in-Publication Data

     Marino, John, date
          Pitchers of perfection / by John Marino.
             p.   cm.
          Includes bibliographical references and index.
          ISBN 1-56799-178-5
            1. Pitchers (Baseball)--United States--Biography.   I. Title.
          GV865.A1M356   1996
          796.357'22'092—dc20
          [B]   95-23804
                                   CIP

Editors: Stephen Slaybaugh and Carrie Smith
Art Director: Jeff Batzli
Designers: Stan Stanski and Kevin Ullrich
Photography Researcher: Samantha Larrance

Color separations by Bright Arts (Singapore) Pte. Ltd.
Printed in China by Leefung-Asco Printers Ltd.

For bulk purchases and special sales, please contact:
Friedman/Fairfax Publishers
Attention: Sales Department
15 West 26th Street
New York, NY 10010
(212) 685-6610 FAX (212) 685-1307

Dedication

To my late mother, Mary, for always correcting my grammar until I got it right, uh, correct; and to my father, George, for always finding time to play catch and sharing his love of the Grand Ol' Game of baseball with me.

Acknowledgments

Thanks to Jack Lang, a longtime force in the Baseball Writers' Association of America, for his anecdotes and helpful insights; the Baseball Hall of Fame in Cooperstown, New York—not the birthplace of baseball, but its eternal, hallowed shrine; the Society of Baseball Research for keeping the flame of studying baseball history forever burning; and all the cooperative librarians in the Twin Cities metro area who patiently and expertly served my research needs. And a special thanks to my editors at Friedman, especially Ben Boyington, whose steady hand and blithe wit made the writing of this book all the more enjoyable.

CONTENTS

The wooden backstop was doing what the over-matched catcher couldn't. The wood, though badly cracked and increasingly splintered, was stopping fastballs thrown by a big, burly Ohio farm kid by the name of Denton True Young.

But the given name of that six-foot-two-inch, 210-pound pitching prospect wouldn't last for long. When Young's tryout with the Cleveland Spiders was finished, an observer compared the wrecked condition of the backstop to the damage done by a cyclone.

Thus a nickname was born and an immortal career was launched.

The name Cy Young has endured in the annals of baseball history, etched not only in the minds of baseball historians but also on the plaque awarded each year to the best all-around pitcher in both the American and National Leagues.

Over the course of his awe-inspiring twenty-two-year career, Cy Young put up numbers deserving of an award named after himself. Upon Young's death in 1955, Major League Baseball Commissioner Ford Frick urged the Baseball Writers' Association of America (BBWAA) to establish the Cy Young Memorial Award. The award has been given annually since 1956 and is now simply called the Cy Young Award.

Young's road to immortality began in 1890, when he embarked on his major league career with the Cleveland Spiders of the National League. By the time he finished his career with the Boston Braves of the National League in 1911 (after stints with the St. Louis Cardinals, Boston Red Sox, and Cleveland Indians), Young had single-handedly rewritten the record books.

Some of his records have been broken, but others are still out of reach. Young's 511 wins are 95 more than "Big Train" Walter Johnson, the number two man on the list, and 148 more than any pitcher in the past half-century has had. His 7,357 innings pitched are more than 1,400 better than his closest pursuer, Jim "Pud" Galvin, who, unlike Young, pitched his entire career with the distance from the pitcher's mound to home plate at 50 feet. And Young, who will always be known as the man who

threw the first World Series pitch, is the only pitcher to win more than 200 games in each league and was the first pitcher to hurl three no-hitters.

Young's contributions to baseball's record books also includes a perfect game, thrown in 1904, when he was thirty-seven. It was the first thrown since the distance from the pitcher's mound to home plate was increased to 60 feet 6 inches in 1893, and only the third perfect game at that point in history. The flawless outing came in the midst of Young's 24-inning hitless streak—a record that still stands. The streak started in the final 2 innings of his start on April 25, followed by 7 innings of hitless relief on April 30. Next came his perfect game on May 5 against the Philadelphia Athletics, and in his next start on May 11, Cy hurled 6 hitless innings before the string was finally snapped.

Every pitcher aspires to obtain the kind of numbers that Cy Young put up during his time on

the pitcher's mound, even for just one season, if not a career; Young's lifetime earned run average totaled an impressive 2.63. Five times he won 30 or more games in a season; fifteen times—including nine years in a row—he won 20 or more games. And sixteen times he pitched 300 or more innings in a season.

The first pitcher to receive the Cy Young Award was 27 game–winner Don Newcombe of the Brooklyn Dodgers. Since that 1956 debut, the award's voting process has undergone some major league revisions.

During Ford Frick's tenure as commissioner, only one pitcher from all of Major League Baseball was chosen to receive the award each year. In 1967, however, a decision was made to name a pitcher from both the American and National Leagues. Following closely behind was the implementing of a new point system in 1970 to avoid ties among winners—a change necessitated by the only tie in the award's history, when Detroit's Denny McLain and Mike Cuellar of Baltimore tied in 1969 with ten votes each.

In the beginning, one beat writer (and member of the BBWAA) who covered a major league team would cast a vote for one pitcher. In 1956 there were sixteen major league teams; thus sixteen votes were cast. Newcombe received ten votes in that inaugural year, while his Dodgers teammate Sal Maglie finished second with four votes. Milwaukee's Warren Spahn and New York Yankee Whitey Ford tied for third with one vote apiece.

In 1961, with the expansion of the American League to ten teams, eighteen votes were cast, a total that increased to twenty the following year when the National League underwent its own expansion. When the dual-winner system was instituted in 1967, the number of voters doubled, going from twenty total to twenty for each league. A year after the Cuellar-McLain tie, a new 5-3-1 system was put into play. The twenty writers in

Opposite: More than eighty years after his retirement, Cy Young's record of 511 career wins remains the most untouchable of any all-time record, in pitching or hitting.

Changes in Pitching Rules

....

In the nineteenth century, there was a flurry of rule changes made, as the keepers of the Grand Ol' Game fine-tuned their new-found plaything.

In 1881, when pitchers were still throwing underhand, the mound-to-plate distance was changed from 45 to 50 feet. In 1893, it was again increased, this time to its current measure of 60 feet 6 inches. When the mound was first pushed back to its present distance, run production increased from just over 3 runs per team per game in 1892 to 4.6 runs per team per game in 1893.

As a result of this change, Cy Young's earned run average went from a league-leading 1.93 in 1892, when he won 36 games, to 3.36 in 1893. Nevertheless, he managed to lead the league with 34 wins.

In 1881, batters had to amass 8 balls for a walk. In 1882, that number was reduced to 7, and in 1884, when pitchers were first allowed to throw overhand, it was further reduced to 6. In 1889, a walk was finally reduced to 4 balls, but not before the rule makers tinkered with the strike count. For the 1887 season, it was decided that if a batter received a called third strike, he would actually be allowed a fourth strike before being called out. That silly rule lasted all of one year.

After 1968, the so-called Year of the Pitcher, baseball's powers-that-be made perhaps the first important change in pitching rules since 1893. They established a maximum mound height of 10 inches. Before the rule was written, mound height was left up to each club's discretion, and mounds all across the big leagues were gradually being made higher and higher, which allowed pitches to attain greater speed as pitchers "fell" off the mound at the end of their windup.

Brooklyn's Don Newcombe, the first Cy Young Award winner in 1956. "Newk" stood tall that year, also winning the National League's MVP Award.

each league continued to choose the pitcher they thought most outstanding, thus earning that pitcher five points. In addition, they cast a vote for a second- and third-place pitcher, thus earning those players three points and one point, respectively.

With so many points to go around, the chances of another tie became very remote. There have been no ties through 1995, but there have been some pretty close decisions during the 5-3-1 era. The closest came in 1987 in the National League when Philadelphia's ace reliever Steve Bedrosian edged Chicago starter Rick Sutcliffe fifty-seven to fifty-five, with San Francisco starter Rick Reuschel not far behind with fifty-four points. The closest decision during the single-vote era that didn't end in a tie was in 1958: New York Yankee Bob Turley nipped Warren Spahn of the Milwaukee Braves five votes to four, while Spahn's teammate Lew Burdette and Bob Friend of Pittsburgh garnered three votes each.

This book takes a look at each Cy Young Award winner, from 1956 through 1995.

Some outstanding pitchers, like Steve Carlton and Greg Maddux, have dominated the Cy Young voting like no others, and thus they share a chapter. Carlton and Maddux are the only four-time winners. And Sandy Koufax, the only repeat recipient from the single-winner era, who won the award three times, each by unanimous acclaim, is given his own chapter.

Three other three-time winners—Jim Palmer, Tom Seaver, and Roger Clemens—share a chapter here, while another is devoted to the four two-time winners: Denny McLain, Bob Gibson, Gaylord Perry, and Bret Saberhagen.

The following chapter contains the remaining winners, a brief discussion of the changing role of the relief pitcher in baseball history, and the shifting attitudes among Cy Young voters toward relievers. The final chapter takes a look at the great and near-great pitchers who never won a Cy Young Award, despite pitching well enough to have perhaps won the award in a less competitive year.

Each Cy Young Award winner receives a plaque, courtesy of the BBWAA, to signify his outstanding season and to keep his name alive in baseball history.

The imposing follow-through of "Rocket Roger," the Boston Red Sox's ace fireballer Roger Clemens.

CHAPTER ONE

The Dynamic Duo: Steve Carlton and Greg Maddux

In four decades of Cy Young Award winners, only two have won the coveted award four times: Steve Carlton and Greg Maddux. No two pitchers could have more contrasting styles.

If you could put power in a bottle, the label would read "Carlton." If you could paint a portrait of a mound surgeon, there would stand Maddux, peering in at his operating table: home plate. However, there is one similarity: both pitchers could control not only their pitches but NL hitters as well.

There the resemblence pretty much ends.

Carlton, on one hand, (and please make that the left hand), was a power pitcher who relied on an explosive fastball and a nasty slider—a slider so nasty, in fact, it has been called the best of all time. Maddux on the other hand, (yes, he's a righty), is the master artisan of finesse. He virtually wields a paintbrush on the mound as he is able to "paint" the corners of home plate, much to the continued amazement of hitters, umpires, and fans.

Before Maddux, no pitcher had ever won more than two straight Cy Young Awards. Greg won his fourth straight in 1995, and who knows what the next years will bring?

STEVE CARLTON

A change of scenery can sometimes be just what a pitcher needs to help jump-start his career. But who would think a 20-game winner needed a career boost?

It seems that was just what Steve Carlton needed. When the strapping, six-foot-five-inch left-hander changed addresses, a good pitcher became a great one.

Above: Carlton fires a pitch in the ninth inning of a game against the Houston Astros in 1980. The Phillies went on to win 2–1 and Carlton earned his fifteenth win. Opposite: Carlton celebrates his twentieth win in 1976 with catcher Tim McCarver and third baseman Mike Schmidt.

At the age of twenty-six, Carlton had won 20 games in 1971 with the St. Louis Cardinals. But a post-season contract dispute and the resulting hard feelings with Cardinal management led to a swap of starters, and Carlton was shipped to Philadelphia, in exchange for Rick Wise.

At first, the deal didn't sit well with the notoriously demanding Phillies fans. The popular Wise had led the last-place Phils in 1971 with 17 wins and a 2.88 earned run average, and after the righthander was traded to St. Louis, he won 16 games in each of the next two seasons for the Redbirds. Good numbers, to be sure, but by the end of the 1972 season, Phillies fans must have been thinking, "Rick who?"

Carlton all but obliterated any memory of Wise with a stellar 27–10 season to win his first of what would be a record four Cy Young Awards. He also demolished the collective confidence of NL hitters, who batted a paltry .206 for the season against the man they called "Lefty."

Carlton's 1972 season was the first time in major league history that a pitcher led in wins despite his team's place in the league's basement. The woeful Phillies brought up the bottom of the six-team Eastern Division by winning a mere 59 games, a full 11 games behind the fifth-place Montreal Expos.

Those extra 7 wins weren't the only noticeable improvement in Carlton's statistics. In 1971, despite logging a 20–9 record for the Redbirds, he had a bulging 3.56 ERA, and hitters teed off against his pitching at a .262 clip. But that was before Carlton perfected his legendary slider. In 1972, blessed with unrelenting control, an already

Carlton ready to deliver another unhittable slider.

explosive fastball, and the addition of a slider to his repertoire, Carlton reeled off one of the best seasons in modern history. While batters flailed at the air, Steve reached rarified heights, spinning a league-leading 1.97 ERA and winning more games in one season than any pitcher in the National League has since accomplished.

Carlton's 27 wins that year tied the NL record for lefthanders, set by Sandy Koufax in 1966. Lefty also earned a most respected reputation as a workhorse, completing 30 of his 41 starts and pitching 346 innings—the most in the league since 1953. His 310 strikeouts again put him in exclusive company with Koufax, as the only NL lefties in history to scale the 300-K plateau. And through it all, Carlton walked only eighty-seven batters, an average of 2.2 per game.

"I feel like we're going to win every time he goes out there," teammate Larry Bowa, the Phillies' All-Star shortstop said that year. "I've never seen a lefthander throw those kinds of curves and sliders."

During the course of his historic season, Carlton won 15 straight games, four short of the single-season mark set by New York Giant Rube Marquard in 1912. Steve's 27 victories constituted 45.8 percent of his team's wins, a percentage unequalled this century in either league.

Besides leading the National League in wins, strikeouts, ERA, innings, and complete games, Carlton also finished second in winning percentage (.730), shutouts (8), fewest hits allowed per nine innings (6.68), and opponents' on-base percentage (.255). His dominance on the mound was accurately reflected in the Cy Young Award voting, where he gathered all twenty-four first-place votes.

As dramatic as Carlton's emergence into the spotlight was, it wasn't totally unexpected. He had shown some promise early in his career with St. Louis, winning 14 games in 1967 and 13 more the following year. But his accomplishments were often overshadowed by a teammate, Hall of Fame pitcher Bob Gibson, who astounded the baseball world in the late 1960s and early '70s.

Perhaps symbolic of Carlton's early career was his record-setting 19-strikeout performance on September 15, 1969, against the New York Mets. Despite breaking a record that had stood since 1938, Carlton lost the game, 4–3, as the Amazin' Mets got two home runs courtesy of the bat of Ron Swoboda. Ironically, in Swoboda's two other plate appearances against Carlton that day, the mighty Met went down swinging.

After the game, Gibson commiserated with his teammate: "Poor Steve," Gibby said sympathetically. "He strikes out nineteen, and he won't be able to sleep tonight."

But the import of the moment wasn't totally lost on Carlton, who was too pumped to wallow in defeat: "It's the best stuff I ever had," he told reporters afterward. "When I had 9 strikeouts, I decided to go all the way; but it cost me the game, because I started to challenge every batter."

Steve struck out the side four times: "I knew I had something special when I got that standing ovation," he said. "That's the first one I ever got." The first of many, many more.

He finished that '69 season with a 17–11 record, 210 strikeouts, and a very good 2.17 ERA—second best in the league. A point better, in fact, than Gibson's 2.18. But it wasn't until he left St. Louis and emerged from his teammate's broad shadow that Lefty finally garnered some major accolades for himself.

After a season like 1972, however, it seemed inevitable that Carlton was doomed to slip a notch or two from his lofty perch. And slip he did, the following year—winning only 13 while being saddled with 20 losses. And he saw his ERA swell to a hefty 3.90. Still, 1973 wasn't a total loss. Lefty once again led the league with 293 innings and fanned a solid 223 batters.

In 1974 Carlton showed signs of resiliency by winning 16 games and leading the league with 240 strikeouts. But 1975 didn't pan out quite as well: he struggled to a 15–14 record, with 192 Ks and a 3.56 ERA, so in the midst of that mediocre season, the Phillies' brass decided something had to be done in order to help Carlton recharge his batteries.

The high-voltage answer came in the form of Carlton's favorite batterymate from his St. Louis days—Tim McCarver, the former All-Star catcher (and now a nationally known television sportscaster).

Coincidentally, McCarver had contacted the Phillies during the 1975 season in the hopes of landing a broadcasting position. Instead, they offered the thirty-four-year-old former Redbird a part-time catching job. With All-Star Bob Boone handling the everyday catching chores, the Phillies didn't need McCarver to plant himself

Quiet Carlton

Steve Carlton, shown here in 1972, has a personality as wily as his slider.

Yes, he's eccentric. Yes, he was quoted to have made anti-Semitic comments that he later denied. And, yes, he didn't talk to the media for eight years!

The discipline and strength of will that allowed Steve Carlton to avoid the media for so long was the same discipline that he showed in his off-season conditioning regimen, which enabled him to continue pitching into his forties. But when he signed with the San Francisco Giants in July 1986, after being released earlier in the year by the Philadelphia Phillies, even Silent Steve had to admit that it was time to talk again.

Presiding over his first press conference in ten years, Carlton admitted, "You can't make a move like this and not talk to the media." Then, as if to assure everyone that he was still a bit of a flake, he predicted that he would continue to pitch until he was fifty. Two and a half years and 17 wins later, his prediction, and his slider, ran out of steam.

While it was his Hall of Fame slider and fastball that baffled opposing hitters, it was Carlton's personality that baffled observers and friends off the field.

"To say that Steve has a difficult time relating is an understatement," said former Carlton teammate and longtime friend Tim McCarver. "I don't understand Lefty. I've known him for three decades and I don't understand him."

A batter's nightmare: the six-foot-five-inch Carlton striding toward home plate with baseball in hand, determination written all over his face, and fire in his eyes.

percentage. He also pared down his ERA to 3.13 and held hitters to a .237 batting average.

Better yet, the rest of the Phillies finally caught up with their stellar teammate and won 101 games, becoming the Eastern Division champions by a 9-game margin. For the first time since 1950, Phillies fans could watch their team in postseason play. And despite eventually losing to the defending world champion Cincinnati Reds in the playoffs in 3 straight games, both Carlton and the Phillies proved to be on the right track for future success.

Carlton continued to put himself through intense workouts, strengthening the arm that was able to put the maximum amount of spin on his renowned slider. With a vicelike grip, made possible by the strength of his powerful forearm, Lefty was able to throw his devastating slider with unprecedented speed and movement. Throughout his twenty-four-year career, opposing batters could muster only a .240 average against his superior stuff, a testament to his conditioning and consistency.

As any personal trainer will advise, building strength and achieving a high level of conditioning involves hard work, dedication, and nutrition. Carlton applied all three: hard work in the weight room, dedication to the martial arts, and lots and lots of rice.

Rice in his diet?

Well, not exactly. Steve didn't actually eat rice to improve his game, but it was very useful stuff in his workouts. Carlton would stick his arm into a big barrel of rice (uncooked, of course) and twist and turn, working the muscles he used to throw his million-dollar slider.

Of course, a heaping helping of talent was also included in Carlton's recipe for success, as he ably demonstrated in 1977. With his game once again cooking on the front burner, Lefty concocted a season worthy of his second Cy Young Award, as the Phillies repeated as Eastern Division champs.

It was five years in the making after his monumental 1972 season, and Phillies fans were beginning to wonder if Steve had it in him to win another Cy Young Award. But 1977 began a six-season span in which Carlton would win three more—permanently cementing his name in pitching history.

With McCarver still behind the plate and the previous season's 20 wins under his belt, Carlton

behind the plate on a daily basis—just every fifth day, when Lefty was twirling his slider. McCarver took the job.

Despite the public's perception of Carlton and McCarver as an odd couple—the taciturn Lefty and the effervescent left-handed-hitting catcher—the chemistry between the two worked,

and the formula began to bubble by the end of the 1975 season.

A rejuvenated Carlton was eager to start the 1976 season on a positive note, and his enthusiasm rang true throughout that bicentennial year. Lefty regained his winning ways and logged a 20–7 record for a league-leading .741 winning took the National League by storm in 1977, winning a league-leading 23 games with a 2.64 ERA (fourth-best in the league) and allowing hitters a .223 average (third-best among NL starters).

Carlton, firmly established as the best left-handed starter in the National League, won 16 and 18 games over the next two seasons, respectively, for a Phillies club that just kept getting better and better. The stage was finally set: 1980 was the year when both Carlton and his team would finally get over the hump and make it to the World Series.

After three straight division titles from 1976 to 1978, the 3 straight playoff losses took their toll. The Phils finished a distant fourth in 1979, 14 games behind the rival Pirates. But a new day in Phillies history dawned along with the new decade, and Carlton was ready. His arm, his confidence, and his arsenal of pitches were as strong as ever, and it was time to take both his game and his team to the next level. By the end of 1980's regular-season play, batters had mustered only a .218 average against Lefty as he led the league with 24 wins, 304 innings, and 286 strikeouts. He was second in the league with 13 complete games and a 2.34 ERA, winning his third Cy Young Award.

In the 1980 NL playoffs against the Houston Astros, Carlton started and won Game One (with relief help from Tug McGraw) and had a no-decision in Game Four, which the Phillies won, 5–3 in 10 innings. The Phils then won Game Five to advance to the World Series. A 6–4 decision gave Carlton his first Series win in Game Two, in which he pitched 8 innings and got relief help from Ron Reed in the ninth. Lefty again proved his worth as a big-money pitcher when he took the hill for the clincher in Game Six, pitching 8 strong innings en route to a 4–1 victory.

It was a memorable season that will forever be etched into the city of Philadelphia's sporting memory. To this day, 1980 is Philly's only World Series victory year. But that year wasn't Carlton's last Cy Young season. Lefty still had one left.

In 1981, baseball experienced its first full-blown players' strike, occurring in midseason and wiping out about 50 games from June to August. Split-season standings were used to determine divisional semifinalists, and an extra round of playoffs was added.

The Phillies won the first half-season and were pitted in the division playoffs against the Montreal Expos. The Expos clinched the best-of-five playoff series when Steve Rogers outpitched Carlton in the fifth game, 3–0. It was a disappointing ending to a solid season in which Lefty logged a 13–4 record, a 2.42 ERA, and 179 strikeouts—just one K behind Dodgers rookie sensation Fernando Valenzuela's league-leading 180. That year Carlton placed third in the Cy Young balloting (after Valenzuela and New York Met Tom Seaver).

However, in 1982, Lefty received twenty of a possible twenty-four first-place Cy Young votes and amassed 112 total points, well ahead of Steve Rogers, who received twenty-nine total points, for second place. That year, Carlton led the league in five major categories, amassing 23 wins, 19 complete games, 6 shutouts, 296 innings, and 286 strikeouts. Not bad for a thirty-seven-year-old power pitcher with more than 4,200 innings and 3,400 strikeouts in the books!

In 1983 the Phillies made it back to the World Series, and Carlton once again led the league with season totals of 284 innings and 275 strikeouts. His record fell to 15–16, despite his holding opponents to a .258 batting average. In the Phillies' 4-game playoff win over the Los Angeles Dodgers, Carlton again proved his worth by spinning 7 shutout innings in a 1–0 Game One win and pitching the 7–2 clincher in Game Four. In the World Series, Carlton also pitched to win, allowing just 5 hits and 2 earned runs in 6⅔ innings. But his teammates couldn't solve the puzzle of the Baltimore Orioles' pitching staff, and the Birds took the world title in 5 games.

Carlton had one more good season left in his incredible arm: in 1984 he logged a 13–7 record in 229 innings, striking out 163 while holding batters to a .246 average. But unfortunately in 1985, age and shoulder trouble finally caught up with Lefty. That year, at the age of forty, he only managed to win 1 game and the Phillies traded him to the San Francisco Giants during the 1986 season. Over the course of the final three seasons of his magnificent career, Carlton pitched briefly for the Chicago White Sox, Cleveland Indians, and Minnesota Twins.

Carlton's career totals are nothing short of awe-inspiring. In addition to his record four Cy Young Awards, he won 329 games, pitched 5,217 innings, struck out 4,136 batters (the second-highest total in history), and fashioned a 3.22 ERA.

1972 NL WINNING STATS

WINS	27
LOSSES	10
PCT.	.730
ERA	1.97
GAMES	41
INNINGS	346.1
HITS	257
BASE ON BALLS	87
STRIKEOUTS	310
SHUTOUTS	8

1977 NL WINNING STATS

WINS	23
LOSSES	10
PCT.	.697
ERA	2.64
GAMES	36
INNINGS	283
HITS	229
BASE ON BALLS	89
STRIKEOUTS	198
SHUTOUTS	2

1980 NL WINNING STATS

WINS	24
LOSSES	9
PCT.	.727
ERA	2.34
GAMES	38
INNINGS	304
HITS	243
BASE ON BALLS	90
STRIKEOUTS	286
SHUTOUTS	3

1982 NL WINNING STATS

WINS	23
LOSSES	11
PCT.	.676
ERA	3.10
GAMES	38
INNINGS	295.2
HITS	253
BASE ON BALLS	86
STRIKEOUTS	286
SHUTOUTS	6

GREG MADDUX

Perhaps a newcomer to baseball might think that Greg Maddux's first name is "First Ever." He was the first pitcher ever to win three straight Cy Youngs. Then he became the first ever to win four in a row.

In the process of winning his fourth straight Cy Young Award, Maddux became only the second pitcher in history to be voted a unanimous winner two years in a row, following in the footsteps of the great Sandy Koufax.

There never was any doubt in 1995: Greg had a 10-game winning streak during the Atlanta Braves' only world championship season. He recorded an astonishing 19–2 record and was the first pitcher since "Big Train" Walter Johnson in 1919 to record sub-1.80 ERAs in consecutive seasons. He walked a scant twenty-three batters in 210 innings. For his career, Maddux has recorded a 150–93 record with an ERA of 2.88.

Greg is so impressive that even his teammate Tom Glavine, himself a Cy Young Award winner, holds the young ace in awe. "It seems like just when you think he's had a career year," Glavine marveled, "he comes back and has a better one. Maybe he'll leave some room for the rest of us to win one some time."

Then again, maybe not.

Nobody threw better in the National League in 1992 than Maddux. During a five-year span, culminating with his first Cy Young Award, Maddux won more games (87) and pitched more innings (1,255) than any hurler in the league. But it wasn't until 1992 that he finally put together all his talent and potential for a convincing Cy Young Award season.

It was a September to remember for Maddux, who was running second in Cy Young consideration to the Atlanta Braves' Tom Glavine, the 1991 winner, for most of the season. By late August, Glavine was 19–3, but then cracked a rib and lost 5 of his final 6 decisions, ending the season at 20–8. Meanwhile, Maddux, who was steady if not spectacular through the season's first five months, went on a tear, winning 5 of his last 6 decisions. It was enough to catapult him past Glavine.

Greg finished the season with a 20–11 record. He went 10–3 with a 1.93 ERA following the All-Star break to finish the year with a 2.18 ERA,

A smooth operator, Maddux was all business on the mound at Wrigley Field when he pitched for the Cubs in 1992.

third-best in the league. He led the league with 268 innings, was second in limiting hitters to a .210 average, and ranked third with 199 strikeouts. And in limiting opponents to 4 or fewer hits in 12 of his 36 starts for the fourth-place Cubs, Maddux became the first pitcher since Randy Jones of the San Diego Padres in 1976 to win the award while playing for a losing team.

It had been a great season for the right-hander, but Maddux had other ideas. "I'd trade it all to play for a winner," he said. "I'd love to play for a contender. That's my top priority." So with Cy Young Award in hand, Greg had the pick of the litter and chose to sign a five-year, $28 million deal with the two-time defending NL champion Atlanta Braves.

In 1993, Maddux duplicated his Cy Young feat, easily outpointing Glavine, now his teammate, and he got his wish. After a slow start, the Braves won their third straight Western Division title, barely outpacing the San Francisco Giants. But much to Maddux's chagrin, the Braves failed in their bid to return to the World Series—they lost to the Philadelphia Phillies in 6 games in the NL playoffs.

That disappointment couldn't diminish Maddux's regular-season numbers. His pinpoint control and nasty split-fingered fastball combined that year for 20 wins and a league-leading 2.36 ERA. Although Glavine had won 22 games, his high 3.20 ERA lost him votes. The Atlanta lefty finished third behind Billy Swift of San Francisco, who won 21 and had a 2.82 ERA. Maddux received twenty-two of the twenty-eight first-place votes to further cement his reputation as the best starting pitcher in the National League.

In 1994, Greg catapulted himself into legendary status by winning 16 games in the strike-shortened season. His 1.56 ERA was the lowest in the majors in nine years.

1992 NL WINNING STATS

WINS	20
LOSSES	11
PCT.	.645
ERA	2.18
GAMES	35
INNINGS	268
HITS	201
BASE ON BALLS	70
STRIKEOUTS	199
SHUTOUTS	4

1993 NL WINNING STATS

WINS	20
LOSSES	10
PCT.	.667
ERA	2.36
GAMES	36
INNINGS	267
HITS	228
BASE ON BALLS	52
STRIKEOUTS	197
SHUTOUTS	1

1994 NL WINNING STATS

WINS	16
LOSSES	6
PCT.	.727
ERA	1.56
GAMES	25
INNINGS	202
HITS	150
BASE ON BALLS	31
STRIKEOUTS	156
SHUTOUTS	3

1995 NL WINNING STATS

WINS	19
LOSSES	2
PCT.	.905
ERA	1.63
GAMES	29
INNINGS	209.2
HITS	147
BASE ON BALLS	23
STRIKEOUTS	181
SHUTOUTS	3

Maddux's ERA

Greg Maddux in the midst of delivering another fiery pitch for the Atlanta Braves.

In 1994, the so-called Year of the Hitter, how do you figure Greg Maddux? He twirled a 1.56 ERA and won 16 games against 6 losses while pitchers all around him were stumbling about with severe cases of shell shock. In the process, he became the first pitcher ever to win three straight Cy Young Awards.

In the strike-shortened 1994 season, NL teams scored an average of 4.65 runs per game and banged out 9.21 hits per game over the approximately 115-game schedule. Along with his minuscule ERA, Maddux allowed an average of only 6.68 hits.

While his union mates were foregoing their baseball incomes, Maddux collected a smart $750,000 bonus for winning his second straight Cy Young Award with the same club. How's that for a contract clause?

And while some people claimed that the BBWAA shouldn't have given out their annual awards because the season had been shortened, Maddux didn't buy that logic: "What do you say to people that think that way?" he said. "I don't have a problem with not being able to make my last 10 starts."

Despite the reduced number of games, and despite having won 20 games in 1993 and having led the National League that year with a 2.36 ERA, Maddux—and many observers—felt that 1994 had clearly been his "best year ever."

CHAPTER TWO

Sandy's Award

Before the commercialized world of professional sports became the haven of hyperbole it is today, there was an athlete deserving of all the grandest adjectives that today's marketing mavens could muster.

From 1962 through 1966, Sandy Koufax was as dominant a pitcher as any in baseball's long history. Although Koufax did receive a great deal of recognition and praise, if he were pitching today the hype machines of Hollywood and Madison Avenue would by now have run out of superlatives.

While pitching for the Los Angeles Dodgers in the early 1960s, "Koo-foo" owned the Cy Young Award. Not only did he win in 1963, 1965, and 1966, but in each of those seasons—all during Commissioner Ford Frick's single-winner era—Koufax was granted pitching's greatest prize by unanimous vote.

If that weren't enough, it's entirely conceivable that this Dodgers' Hall of Fame hurler could have won five Cy Youngs in a row, if not for two serious injuries that cut short his 1962 and 1964 seasons. In 1962, he suffered from a circulatory problem in the index finger of his throwing hand, while a deep bruise to his elbow abruptly ended his 1964 campaign in August.

To put his career accomplishments in perspective, consider this: of the fifty pitchers who have won the Cy Young Award since its inception in 1956, nine have been unanimous winners, but only Koufax was named on all ballots during the one-pitcher era. And no other pitcher has ever been elected unanimously more than once.

During his heyday, Koufax dominated hitters like no other pitcher before or since. He is the undisputed standard-setter for all future generations of pitchers, winning 111 games in that half-decade, despite missing nearly 20 starts because of injuries. He won 77 percent of his decisions and maintained season averages of 275 innings and 289 strikeouts. And during his last two seasons, he

Sandy Koufax at work. Will he throw an explosive fastball, or a curveball that drops a foot? Sandy kept them guessing. Here, he shows his winning form in Game Seven of the 1965 World Series.

pitched in continual pain, hampered by an arthritic left elbow that eventually forced his early retirement in 1966.

A skeptic unfamiliar with Koufax's career might assume that his impressive numbers came against a weak-hitting National League. On the contrary, year in and year out, Koufax faced some of the toughest hitters in major league his-

tory. The sixties were years loaded with some of the game's greatest power hitters in the prime of their careers and many others who hit for high averages, including career home run leader Hank Aaron, the incomparable Willie Mays, the powerful and dangerous Frank Robinson, the career hit leader Pete Rose, the remarkable Roberto Clemente, the explosive

Willie McCovey, and the always incredible Orlando Cepeda.

All had their shots at Koufax and even won a few battles. But over the long haul, it was Sandy who won the war. Koufax dominated with an explosive fastball and a devastating curveball that hitters and commentators alike compared to a ball "falling off a table," breaking sharply and with little warning. While a batter had to protect himself against the great Koufax heater, he usually didn't have enough time to adjust to the sharply downward-breaking curve.

Sandy still holds the NL season strikeout record of 382, and no pitcher has yet to equal his five consecutive league ERA titles. The only other pitcher in history to wear more than two straight ERA crowns is Lefty Grove, holder of the AL record of four straight, set from 1929 to 1932. Not even the legendary Cy Young, nor the dominant Walter Johnson, nor even the other early-twentieth-century greats Grover Cleveland Alexander and Christy Mathewson ever won more than two in a row. And in the years since Koufax's feat, only one pitcher—Roger Clemens of the Boston Red Sox—has won 3 ERA titles in a row.

In 1961 Koufax broke Mathewson's NL strikeout mark of 267 by fanning 269. It was a record that had stood since 1903. Two years later, Sandy broke his own mark by setting down 306 befuddled batters. And two years after that, in 1965, Koufax's 382 Ks smashed Bob Feller's 1946 major league mark of 348. (Sandy's major league record of 382 has since been eclipsed by American Leaguer Nolan Ryan's 383, set in 1973.)

By passing Mathewson in 1961, Koufax alerted the baseball world that his long-talked-about potential was finally being realized. He had always had the talent. Scouts, coaches, and his manager, Walter Alston, knew that Koufax could throw a blazing fastball, but his control was horrible. He was consistently "wild high," a " thrower" rather than a "pitcher."

It was also a case of Koufax not getting the work at the minor league level that he needed in order to feel comfortable on a major league mound—all because of a legal technicality.

Finally over his wildness, the mature Koufax (shown here at 1962 spring training) dominated hitters and Cy Young voting like no other.

1963 NL WINNING STATS

WINS	25
LOSSES	5
PCT.	.833
ERA	1.88
GAMES	40
INNINGS	311
HITS	214
BASE ON BALLS	58
STRIKEOUTS	306
SHUTOUTS	11

....

1965 NL WINNING STATS

WINS	26
LOSSES	8
PCT.	.765
ERA	2.04
GAMES	43
INNINGS	335.2
HITS	216
BASE ON BALLS	71
STRIKEOUTS	382
SHUTOUTS	8

....

1966 NL WINNING STATS

WINS	27
LOSSES	9
PCT.	.750
ERA	1.73
GAMES	41
INNINGS	323
HITS	241
BASE ON BALLS	77
STRIKEOUTS	317
SHUTOUTS	5

Koufax was a "bonus baby"—as players who signed for a large bonus and were first-round draft picks were known—and league rules prevented the Dodgers from farming such players out to the minors. Thus, in his first six seasons in the bigs, Sandy compiled an anemic 36–40 record. He pitched only 42 innings in 1955, his rookie year, and another 59 in 1956, when the Dodgers were still in Brooklyn. Over the next four years, he averaged 148 innings per season but was still over-throwing, trying to get every hitter out with his 96-mile-per-hour fastball.

But in 1961, Koufax turned the corner from promise to performance. It began in spring training, when he hurled 7 no-hit innings against the Minnesota Twins. Then, in his next start in the exhibition season, he hurled 9 innings—his first-ever complete game —and beat the Twins again, 7–3. Before surrendering a ninth-inning 3-run homer in that game, he had pitched 22 consecutive scoreless innings.

Finally, all the good advice from the Dodger's staff that Koufax had previously allowed to go in one ear and out the other had started to stay bottled up inside his head and began to soak into his brain. "It took me six years to get it through my thick skull, but I'm not taking such a big windup," Koufax told reporters at the Dodgers' spring training complex in Vero Beach, Florida. "I'm throwing easier, and I have my confidence now."

That growing confidence spelled doom and gloom for NL hitters for the next half-dozen years.

To go along with 1961's strikeout record, Koufax won 18 games that year, and although his 3.52 ERA wasn't among the league leaders, it was an improvement from his 3.91 mark the year before.

In 1962, Sandy had 216 strikeouts in 184 innings and looked to be well on his way to breaking his own record. But a finger injury put an abrupt end to a season in which he was on pace to pitch 300 innings. If he had continued at the same fanning rate, he would have struck out 352 by year's end. He did, however, begin his string of ERA titles with a tidy 2.54, a mark he would stay below for the rest of his career.

Koufax pitched the 1963 season injury-free. He finally put everything together: health, experience, and "stuff." The end result was a 25–5 record, an NL-record 306 strikeouts, a league-leading 11 shutouts, a minuscule 1.88 ERA, and a stingy .189 batting average against him.

Koufax capped his incredible regular season that year with a World Series performance against the New York Yankees made for the ages. His dominating performance in Game One set the tone for the rest of the Dodgers pitching staff, who allowed just 1 run over the next 3 games in record-

Pitching in his last World Series game, Koufax strides off Dodger Stadium's high mound in Game Two. He lost 6–0 as Los Angeles was swept by Baltimore in 1966.

The Big Holdout

....

Don Drysdale (left) and Sandy Koufax (second from right) posing with the rest of the Dodgers starting rotation.

In 1965, Sandy Koufax and Don Drysdale were the Los Angeles Dodgers' lefty-righty, one-two punch, combining for 49 regular-season wins and another 3 in their triumphant World Series.

Each pitcher earned about $70,000 that year. The Dodgers offered Koufax, a unanimous Cy Young Award winner, a $30,000 raise; Drysdale, winner of 23 regular-season games and another in the Fall Classic, was offered a $15,000 pay hike. Agreeing that this was not nearly high enough, the pitchers decided to form a two-man union and hired Koufax's lawyer, J. William Hayes, to represent them in salary negotiations.

The pair's asking price was a cool half-million dollars each over three years. Dodgers General Manager Buzzy Bavasi countered by offering one-year deals to both pitchers, an additional $5,000 to Koufax, and another $10,000 to Big Don.

Nothing doing, they said. There is strength in numbers, after all, even if "numbers" meant only the two of them—a far cry from today's union solidarity. As leverage, Hayes inked a deal with Paramount Pictures to have both hurlers "act" in a movie called *Warning Shot.* Drysdale was slated to portray a television commentator (foreshadowing the career move he would make after retiring from baseball), while Koufax was to portray a detective.

As April neared and neither pitcher was to be found anywhere near the Dodgers training camp, there was talk that both would sit out the entire 1966 season—a threat that was probably more posturing than anything else. Finally, on March 30, Sandy and Don ended their thirty-two-day holdout and each signed a one-year contract—Koufax for a reported $120,000 (just $10,000 less than Willie Mays, the 1965 MVP and the game's highest-paid player), Drysdale for $105,000.

When asked which of the two pitchers was more relieved to be signed, Bavasi said, "I am."

Paramount released the pitchers from their contracts and Koufax went on to win 27 games, his fifth straight ERA crown, and his third unanimous Cy Young Award in four years. Drysdale, however, slumped to 13–16. "This was the most trying thing that ever happened to me," he said.

ing one of the most surprising sweeps in World Series history.

Sandy began Game One by striking out the first five Yankees he faced and went on to fan a record fifteen batters, in the end outdueling the great Whitey Ford, 5–2. In Game Four, he clinched the Dodgers' second world championship in five years by again outdueling Ford, 2–1, allowing only 6 hits and striking out eight batters. When it was all over, Koufax had set a World Series record, with 23 Ks in a 4-game series.

As dominating as he was in 1963, Sandy looked to be on course to put up even better numbers in 1964, until his elbow injury ended his season in late August. At the time, he had been leading the league in four major categories—19 wins (with only 5 losses), a 1.74 ERA, 7 shutouts, and 223 strikeouts—and he was on a pace to fan 315 batters. Despite missing his final dozen or so starts, at season's end, Sandy still led the league in shutouts and ERA.

It may be hard to imagine any pitcher improving on the kind of numbers that Koufax recorded in 1963, but 1965 was another amazing year for him. Perhaps being sidelined against his will was a motivating factor for Sandy, who seemed to approach 1965 with a renewed determination to pick up where he left off before his injury.

He outperformed the rest of the league in nine major categories, led by his 26 wins, a number tying the NL record for lefties set in 1912 by Rube Marquard and matched in 1936 by Carl Hubbell. Also tops were his .765 winning percentage, 336 innings, 27 complete games, major league–record 382 strikeouts, 10.2 strikeouts per game, 2.04 ERA, positively greedy .179 opponents' batting average, and 5.8 hits per game.

And that wasn't all. Koufax also set a major league record by pitching his fourth no-hitter, a perfect game in which he struck out fourteen, including the final six batters. Nolan Ryan has since surpassed Koufax with an incredible 7 no-hitters—6 in the American League, 4 with the California Angels and 2 with the Texas Rangers, and 1 in the National League, with the Houston Astros. Ryan holds both the AL and the major league record, but Koufax is still the holder of the NL record.

"Sandy was throwing much faster at the end than at the beginning," Dodgers catcher Jeff Torborg told reporters that day. "At the end, he really wanted it, and he was bearing down hard."

And Koufax's star didn't stop rising at the end of the regular season. In the 1965 World Series, he put together a string of 18 innings to rival any of the great postseason performances.

After losing Game Two, when he gave up 6 hits and 2 runs in 6 innings to the powerful Minnesota Twins, Koufax was called upon to pitch Game Five. He responded with a 4-hit shutout in a 7–0 subduing of the mighty Twins lineup that included Harmon Killebrew, Bob Allison, Don Mincher, Tony Oliva, Earl Battey, and 1965's AL Most Valuable Player, Zoilo Versalles.

Only two days' rest followed before Koufax was called to start the decisive Game Seven. Helped by an outstanding fielding play by third baseman Jim Gilliam in the fifth inning, Sandy again turned back the powerful Twins, this time on a 3-hit shutout; the Dodgers won the game, 2–0.

Most pitchers today would have trouble throwing 7 effective innings on three days' rest, but with just those two days, Koufax nevertheless recorded 10 strikeouts, allowed only three walks and retired fourteen of the last fifteen batters he faced in the game. For the Series, he struck out a then-record twenty-nine.

As awesome as Koufax was in 1965, his amazing feats of power and precision didn't end with the Dodgers' latest triumph. There was one more season left in Sandy's ailing arm. In 1966, Koufax won 27 games, an NL record for lefties (later tied by Steve Carlton). He again led the league in a slew of categories: 27 complete games, 5 shutouts, 323 innings, 317 strikeouts, 8.8 strikeouts per game, and a 1.73 ERA.

In the 1966 World Series, however, Koufax was undone by 6 errors in Game Two, and even the great Dodgers pitching staff couldn't defeat an even greater Baltimore Orioles pitching staff. The Birds swept the Series in 4 games.

On November 18, 1966, Sandy Koufax, only thirty years old, called a press conference in Los Angeles to announce his retirement from his beloved baseball, to which he had given so much.

"There's no cure, and it isn't getting any better," Koufax said of his ailing elbow. "And I'm no masochist. I don't enjoy pain. I'll stand it because it's necessary to accomplish a goal, but there will come a point when I won't take it anymore."

And when that point was finally reached, Koufax left baseball as quickly as one of his fastballs exploding into the strike zone.

Upon retiring (because of an arthritic elbow), Koufax stated that he wanted to quit while he "could still comb his hair."

Three's Company: Jim Palmer, Tom Seaver, and Roger Clemens

Whoever coined the phrases "Good things come in threes" and "Third time's a charm" must have had a premonition of Cy Young Award winners. Since 1967, when the award was handed to one pitcher in each league each year (in other words, the post-Koufax era), there have been exactly three pitchers who have won the award exactly three times.

Moreover, the recipients of this unusual triple play—Jim Palmer, Tom Seaver, and Roger Clemens—are all right-handed pitchers renowned for their outstanding control. It's worth taking a look at their careers while they still comprise this unique triumvirate because in any given year, Clemens—still active and still very capable—could join the rank of Steve Carlton and Greg Maddux, and become the game's third four-time winner.

JIM PALMER

Young baseball fans won't remember Jim Palmer's nineteen-year career with the Baltimore Orioles, but it's a safe bet they know him as an underwear salesman. But long before he parlayed his handsome face and well-sculpted physique into a successful commercial career, Palmer was weaving his magic on the mound in the American League with an assortment of pitches.

Using an effective curve, a slider, and a change-up to set up a fastball thrown with pinpoint control, Palmer won 20 or more games in eight seasons and compiled a lifetime total of 268.

He first grabbed Cy Young glory in 1973 when he put together a 22–9 record while leading the AL with a 2.40 earned run average. His pitching that year helped the Orioles win the Eastern Division pennant by an 8-game margin.

Palmer continued his dominance of AL hitters in the 1973 playoffs, shutting out the defending world champion Oakland A's in 5 hits, 6–0, in Game One.

He was no stranger to postseason play, having outdueled Sandy Koufax in Game Two of the 1966 World Series at the tender age of twenty. Palmer pitched a 4-hit shutout to beat Koufax, 6–0. The legendary Los Angeles Dodgers fireballer was undone that day by 6 errors.

In the 1973 playoffs, however, the Oakland A's finally solved the riddle of the Palmer method in Game Four, chasing Jim from the contest in the second inning with 3 runs. The Orioles came back to win the game, 5–4, and forced a deciding Game Five. Palmer pitched briefly in relief in that final outing, but Oakland, a juggernaut in the midst of winning three straight world championships from 1972 to 1974, was not to be denied.

In 1975, Palmer pitched like a man on a mission, and claimed his second Cy Young honor. After missing the better part of the 1974 season with an elbow injury that resulted in a 7–12 record, Palmer returned the next year to his Hall of Fame form. He led the league in his comeback season with 23 wins, 10 shutouts, and a sparkling 2.09 ERA. In addition, Palmer held opposing bat-

Above: The lanky Palmer hid the ball well from the batters behind his high leg kick. Opposite: With a smooth and compact follow-through, Palmer avoided putting added strain on his arm. The result was a career in which he pitched more than 3,900 major league innings.

Baseball's "Odd Couple"—Jim Palmer and Earl Weaver

•••••••••••••••••••••••••••••••

It was early July 1971, and the Baltimore Orioles, who should have been blowing away the rest of the Eastern Division, were only 3½ games ahead of the second-place Boston Red Sox.

It was enough to make the normally abrasive Earl Weaver truly obnoxious. "Don't turn away from me when I talk to you," the irrepressible Orioles manager bellowed at the back of his star pitcher, Jim Palmer, as the lanky right-hander made his way to the watercooler.

It was the ninth inning, and Palmer, who didn't hear Weaver the first time, had 14 strikeouts in a 2–2 duel with Cleveland's lefty ace, Sam McDowell. Five minutes earlier, Weaver had sent his pitching coach, George Bamberger, to the mound to check on Palmer.

"I'm exhausted," Palmer had said. In the Orioles dugout at Cleveland's Municipal Stadium, he was asked how he was doing again. "Well," he answered, "if I was tired five minutes ago, it seems to me I'm still tired."

It was not the answer for which Weaver waited. "Get the hell out of here," Earl screamed, and sent in a pinch hitter for Palmer, who was due up third in the inning. (Remember, this was two years before the designated hitter rule was established in the American League.)

The Orioles bullpen allowed the winning run in the bottom of the ninth, prompting a thirty-five-minute closed-door session between manager and pitcher in the clubhouse. Weaver was irate because he felt that if Palmer had not "ignored" him, the pitcher wouldn't have been thrown out and victory would have belonged to the Orioles.

Weaver and Palmer were truly Major League Baseball's "Odd Couple." While the crusty, curmudgeonly manager and the handsome Hall of Fame pitcher engaged in many a battle, they also came together to win a good number of games.

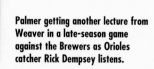
Palmer getting another lecture from Weaver in a late-season game against the Brewers as Orioles catcher Rick Dempsey listens.

Above to opposite, right: Jim Palmer utilized his smooth pitching delivery to blank the Los Angeles Dodgers in Game Two of the 1966 World Series, becoming the youngest player to pitch a Series shutout.

ters to a stingy .216 average that year and also showed his durability by pitching an astonishing 323 innings.

If there were any lingering doubts or fears of new injuries, Palmer dismissed them completely in 1976, when he led the league with 22 wins and 315 innings. And just for good measure, he won another Cy Young Award, becoming just the third pitcher in history to win back-to-back awards.

Despite his three honors, Palmer never earned the same type of reputation as did Tom Seaver or Roger Clemens, both of whom became famous for their consistently overpowering pitching. While Palmer struck out his share of batters—a lifetime total of 2,212—he did it more with finesse than pure power. He was as cerebral as he was athletic.

Palmer's trademark motion—expansive and sweeping, with a high leg kick—proved to be a distraction to hitters. He delivered the ball with such grace and ease that hitters became lulled into a false sense of security. Then, when they least

1973 AL WINNING STATS		1975 AL WINNING STATS		1976 AL WINNING STATS	
WINS	22	WINS	23	WINS	22
LOSSES	9	LOSSES	11	LOSSES	13
PCT.	.710	PCT.	.676	PCT.	.629
ERA	2.40	ERA	2.09	ERA	2.51
GAMES	38	GAMES	39	GAMES	40
INNINGS	296	INNINGS	323	INNINGS	315
HITS	225	HITS	253	HITS	255
BASE ON BALLS	113	BASE ON BALLS	80	BASE ON BALLS	84
STRIKEOUTS	158	STRIKEOUTS	193	STRIKEOUTS	159
SHUTOUTS	6	SHUTOUTS	10	SHUTOUTS	6

expected it, there was Palmer's fastball—already exploding into the catcher's mitt. And usually it was a first-pitch strike, thus putting the batter in an immediate hole.

"I almost never started a hitter off with a breaking pitch," Palmer once explained, "because I couldn't get it over for a strike. You throw what you can for a strike, and you've got the advantage."

After that first pitch, it was anybody's guess—except Palmer's, of course—as to what pitch he would next pull out of his bag of tricks. Even long-

time Orioles manager Earl Weaver was sometimes mystified, and their arguments concerning pitching are legendary. With such good control of his fastball, Palmer would usually try to "paint the corners"—throw strikes by catching as little of home plate as was humanly possible.

Such a tendency would drive Weaver nuts. He'd accuse Palmer of being too fine. "Those pitches are so perfect," Weaver would say, "the hitter won't swing at them and the umpire won't call them strikes."

Weaver often vented his wrath on the umpires, who, the manager complained, would call Palmer's big breaking curveball a ball more often than a strike. Weaver insisted that the big sweeping motion of Palmer's curve would lead the pitch into the strike zone at the last possible second, often after an umpire "gave up" on it.

Palmer, ever the unwilling disciple as half of baseball's "Odd Couple" of the seventies, just did it his way—and pitched himself into the Hall of Fame.

TOM SEAVER

Before Tom Seaver introduced his unique lexicon of pitching terms to devotees of the Grand Ol' Game, a fastball was a fastball. Once "Tom Terrific" waxed eloquent, however, a fastball became a pitch thrown with great "velocity." Before Seaver, a pitcher had good control; after Seaver, a pitcher had effective "location" on his pitches. A fastball used to have pop; now it had "good movement."

Yes, Tom Seaver could really talk a good game, but he could pitch an even better one. His career totals of 311 wins, 61 shutouts, 3,640 strikeouts, and a 2.86 ERA are eloquent testimony to that fact.

A student of the game of baseball and of the art of pitching, Seaver was holding forth on the verities of his chosen craft whenever he wasn't sending strikeout victims back to the dugout.

And no wonder: Seaver was schooled by Rod Dedeaux of the University of Southern California, one of the greatest college coaches of all time. And he earned Rookie of the Year honors in 1967 with the New York Mets, a franchise noted for teaching good pitching techniques.

"Mechanics," he used to say. Every aspect of a pitcher's windup and delivery could be reduced to a discussion of mechanics.

Indeed, a dirt smudge on Seaver's right knee spoke volumes. When Seaver went through his windup, he literally pushed off the pitching rubber with all the force his strong back leg could muster. The right-hander's right leg would spring forward with such force that it would thrust his knee downward, causing it to drag along the dirt of the pitcher's mound.

That dirty knee was a familiar sight throughout Seaver's twenty-year career, and when his pants leg was smudged, it was a clear sign that his mechanics were sound.

In his first Cy Young season of 1969, Seaver and his New York Mets teammates astounded the baseball and nonbaseball worlds alike by winning the World Series, just one year after finishing in ninth place in the National League.

In the Miracle of 1969, Tom Terrific flirted with perfection on July 10 against the Cubs in Shea Stadium. After retiring the first twenty-five batters, Seaver finished with a one-hit shutout. Here, he delivers to Ron Santo in the eighth inning.

Seaver displays perfect form as he drags his right knee along the ground.

Five times in their first seven seasons as an NL expansion team, the Mets finished at the bottom of the ten-team league. Only twice—in 1966 when they won a team-record 66 games, and in 1968, when they improved that record to 73 wins—had the Mets escaped the basement.

But in 1969, Seaver, with his talent and boundless, youthful enthusiasm, led the charge to first place in their division, where the Mets would reside all season. At the same time, at least according to Mr. Terrific, there was another tenant in New York who helped the Mets' cause.

"God is alive and well and has an apartment in Manhattan," the cocky, brash Seaver claimed. Heck, anything was possible. Even the Mets winning their division? Well, most Mets fans agreed earlier in the season not to get carried away. But when September rolled around, even the most hardened New York skeptic had to agree that something very special was happening at Shea Stadium.

The Mets, who had trailed the Chicago Cubs by 9½ games on August 14, won 22 of their next 28 games to pass the Cubs on September 10.

Seaver played a major role in that winning streak. He was 6–0 in September, en route to a league-leading 25 wins against just 7 losses for a .781 winning percentage—the best in the league. He also led the league by holding opponents to a .207 batting average and allowing just 6.7 hits per game.

But more important than just numbers was Seaver's irrepressible optimism and will to win, which infected the Mets' clubhouse and dugout. Seemingly average players were reaching new heights of performance as the lowly Mets were creating miracles on the field. Seaver's role as a team leader nearly won him the league's Most Valuable Player Award; he finished a close second to San Francisco's Willie McCovey, who had a monster year at the plate and received 265 votes to Seaver's 243. In the Cy Young voting, however, Seaver was nearly a unanimous choice, with twenty-three votes. Atlanta Brave Phil Niekro, a 23-game winner that year, got the remaining vote.

In the 1969 World Series, Seaver was saddled with the Mets' only loss, 4–1, in Game One, but he came back in Game Four to pitch a masterful 10 innings for a 2–1 win, allowing only 6 hits.

Four years later, in 1973, Seaver added another Cy Young plaque to his collection by winning 19 games and leading the Mets to another division title. That season, he also led the league with 18 complete games, fewest hits allowed per start (6.8), 251 strikeouts, and lowest batting average allowed (.206).

Seaver then pitched the Mets past the heavily favored Cincinnati Reds in the NL playoffs by winning Game Five, 7–2. Seaver also pitched well enough to win his two World Series starts, but ultimately came up empty each time against the defending world champion Oakland A's. Despite the fact that Seaver allowed only 4 earned runs in 15 innings, Tom's teammates weren't so terrific in the batter's box. He had a no-decision in a 3–2, 11-inning loss in Game Three and came up on the short end of a 3–1 loss in Game Six. Had the Mets won Game Six, it would have clinched their second World Series title in five years, but instead Oakland made it two World Series titles in a row with a 5–2 win in Game Seven.

Over the next two years, Seaver's career mirrored that of Jim Palmer. In 1974, he suffered from injuries—lower-back and hip pain—and slid to 11–11, but he returned with an outstanding campaign in 1975 to win his third Cy Young Award. Unlike his previous disappointing season, he led the league in wins with a 22–9 record.

Along with his explosive fastball, Seaver had now perfected a "circle change." By gripping the ball with his thumb and forefinger in the shape of a circle, he could still generate the same body motion and arm speed that he used in order to throw a fastball, but the looser grip took some speed off the pitch, thus deceiving batters.

The fastball–circle change combination, added to Seaver's typical array of curves and sliders, led to a league-leading 243 strikeouts in 1975. Batters that year could muster only a .214 average against Seaver, who spun a terrific 2.38 ERA.

During the 1977 season, Seaver was traded to Cincinnati, much to the dismay and disgust of Mets fans. Over the next ten years, he won 150 games, mostly for the Reds and White Sox, but also pitched another season for the Mets in 1983. He ended his career after the 1986 season with the Boston Red Sox, having amassed over 300 career wins.

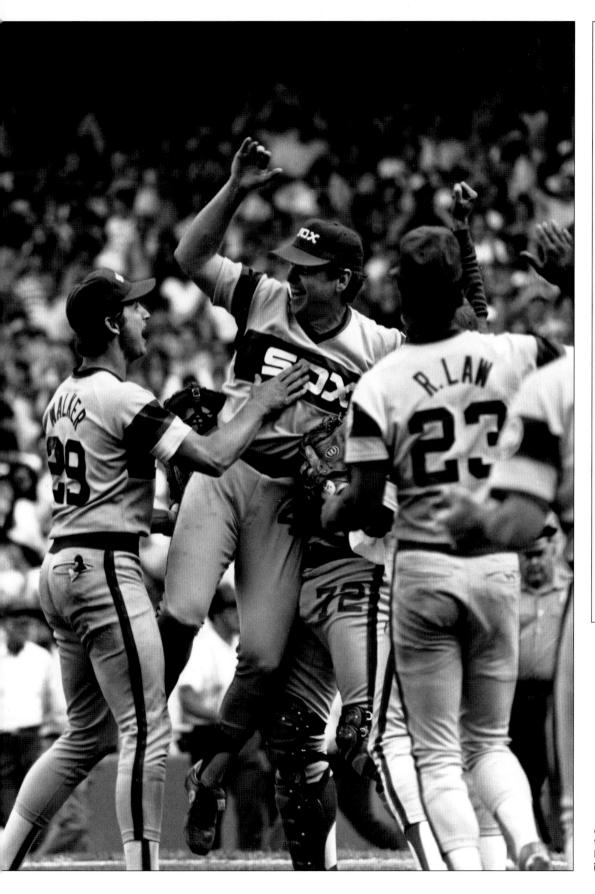

1969 NL WINNING STATS

WINS	25
LOSSES	7
PCT.	.781
ERA	2.21
GAMES	36
INNINGS	273.1
HITS	202
BASE ON BALLS	82
STRIKEOUTS	208
SHUTOUTS	5

1973 NL WINNING STATS

WINS	19
LOSSES	10
PCT.	.655
ERA	2.08
GAMES	36
INNINGS	290
HITS	219
BASE ON BALLS	64
STRIKEOUTS	251
SHUTOUTS	3

1975 NL WINNING STATS

WINS	22
LOSSES	9
PCT.	.710
ERA	2.38
GAMES	36
INNINGS	280
HITS	217
BASE ON BALLS	88
STRIKEOUTS	243
SHUTOUTS	5

Although Seaver had been traded to the White Sox, it was fitting that he won his historic 300th game while pitching in New York. Here, he celebrates his milestone after a 4–1 win over the Yankees in Yankee Stadium.

ROGER CLEMENS

Roger Clemens burst onto the scene in much the same way his fastball explodes into the strike zone. How else could he have earned the nickname "Rocket Man"?

Like a rocket, his ascent was swift. In June 1983, he pitched the University of Texas to the NCAA national championship. By August 1984, Clemens had set a Boston Red Sox rookie record by striking out fifteen batters in 1 game, and was named AL Pitcher of the Month. He finished his inaugural season with a 9–4 record and 126 strikeouts in 133 innings.

But like an ill-fated space mission, Clemens experienced his own personal crash and burn. An arm injury in 1985 put him on the disabled list after only 98 innings. In August he underwent shoulder surgery.

All eyes among Red Sox fans were on the young rocket launcher as 1986 began. Would the young phenomenon live up to his earlier promise or would he fizzle—just another hard thrower who couldn't make it in cozy Fenway

Gritty determination brought Roger Clemens back from shoulder surgery in 1985.

Park, where the famed left-field wall, the Green Monster, is just 315 feet away?

Clemens answered all the skeptics beyond a shadow of a doubt early in the season with a record 20-strikeout performance against the Seattle Mariners, and he finished off any lingering doubts with the kind of season most pitchers only dream of—a season that would earn him a unanimous decision in that year's Cy Young balloting.

Clemens clearly had plenty of solid fuel left in his right arm. He won 24 games (including his first 14 decisions), lost only 4, led the league with a 2.48 ERA, and allowed a league-low .195 batting average in that 1986 season.

Among his other honors that year, he started and won the All-Star Game and was named the day's MVP for pitching 3 no-hit, shutout innings. But the MVP accolades didn't stop there. As winner of the American League's Most Valuable Player Award of 1986, Clemens easily out-pointed New York's Don Mattingly by a total of 339–258, while Roger's teammate Jim Rice finished third with 241 points.

The only disappointment for Clemens in 1986 was the Red Sox's failure to win the World Series, despite being within 1 strike of beating the favored New York Mets. In the 1986 Classic, Clemens started 2 games for the Sox, but lasted only 11⅓ innings, with no decisions.

Despite the disappointing end to a glorious season and the Red Sox's subsequent slip to fifth place in 1987, Clemens resumed his dominance of AL hitters with another sterling performance. He became only the fourth pitcher in history to win back-to-back Cy Young Awards.

His 20–9 record constituted a .690 win-loss percentage, the best in the league. His 20 wins were tops, as were his 18 complete games and 7 shutouts.

At age twenty-five, Clemens had cemented his reputation as the dominant pitcher in the American League, and merely embellished it four years later in 1991 when he won his third Cy Young Award.

Just like a rocket, Clemens's third Cy Young season came in stages—three, to be exact. The first stage was a perfect liftoff to begin the season at 5–0 with an infinitesimal 0.66 ERA, including 3 straight shutouts. Writers and fans were all but handing him the Cy Young Award in May, along with the MVP Award—the Red Sox were in first place.

Poised to go into orbit, Roger's second stage turned sour as he struggled with a bout of food

1986 AL WINNING STATS	
WINS	24
LOSSES	4
PCT.	.857
ERA	2.48
GAMES	33
INNINGS	254
HITS	179
BASE ON BALLS	67
STRIKEOUTS	238
SHUTOUTS	1

1987 AL WINNING STATS	
WINS	20
LOSSES	9
PCT.	.690
ERA	2.97
GAMES	36
INNINGS	281.2
HITS	248
BASE ON BALLS	83
STRIKEOUTS	256
SHUTOUTS	7

1991 AL WINNING STATS	
WINS	18
LOSSES	10
PCT.	.643
ERA	2.62
GAMES	35
INNINGS	271.1
HITS	219
BASE ON BALLS	65
STRIKEOUTS	241
SHUTOUTS	4

poisoning. Simply put, the Rocket sputtered, went 3–5, and began to doubt himself. Beantown began to wonder, "What's wrong with Roger?" The Rocket's descent prompted one sportswriter to remark, "When Roger Clemens gets a headache, all of Boston takes two aspirin."

During the third and final stage, however, Clemens righted himself, went into a smooth orbit, and put up the same kind of numbers that had made him seem unhittable in April and May.

What was the key to his turnaround? More fastballs. Clemens lives and dies by the fastball, and somehow he had gotten away from what he did best. Once he returned to his bread-and-

Sometimes Clemens seems this close to batters when he launches his patented fastball with his powerful right arm.

butter pitch, the wins once again began to fall into place.

Down the stretch, as the Red Sox found themselves in a pennant race, Clemens logged a 6–0 record with a 1.33 ERA. His winning streak was finally broken on October 1, when he was tagged by the Detroit Tigers for 13 hits and 6 runs. By then the Sox were out of the race, but

Clemens' run had clinched his third Cy Young Award as he led the league with 241 strikeouts and a 2.62 ERA. In his turnaround season, he won 18 games, pitched 271 innings, threw 13 complete games, and walked only sixty-five batters.

While Clemens felt honored at becoming a three-time winner, he tried to keep winning the award in perspective. "You could really get your-

self wrapped up in it if you're a selfish person," he told reporters. "But what everybody has to remember is you have great years so it makes it easier for your team to win. It's no fun doing it for yourself if other people can't share in it."

All of Boston is waiting to share in Roger's next Cy Young season. Most Red Sox fans think it's just a matter of time.

Encore Performers

Only four pitchers have doubled their Cy Young pleasure, winning the big award twice: Denny McLain, Bob Gibson, Gaylord Perry, and Bret Saberhagen.

DENNY MCLAIN AND BOB GIBSON

Both Denny McLain, who pitched for the Detroit Tigers, and Bob Gibson, a Hall of Famer with the St. Louis Cardinals, won their first Cy Young Awards in 1968, the well-documented Year of the Pitcher. How dominant were the masters of the mound that year? Consider these facts:

• Carl Yastrzemski of the Boston Red Sox led the American League with a .301 batting average. The league batting average was .230, the lowest in history.

• Only five National Leaguers hit over the .300 mark: Pete Rose, Matty Alou, Felipe Alou, Alex Johnson, and Curt Flood.

• The National League beat the American League, 1–0, in the All-Star Game in Houston, as the teams combined for a new low of 8 hits. At one point, NL pitchers retired twenty batters in a row.

• Don Drysdale of the Los Angeles Dodgers pitched 6 straight shutouts and a then-record 58 consecutive scoreless innings.

• Denny McLain's 31 wins marked the first 30-win season in the major leagues since 1934 and only the fourth since 1920. No one has won 30 games since McLain.

• Bob Gibson pitched 5 straight shutouts, and his 1.12 earned run average was the third-lowest in major league history in the years since the inception of the 60-foot-6-inch pitching distance.

• The low batting averages and even lower ERAs prompted the Rules Committee to take some of the advantage away from the pitchers. They voted to lower the mound for the 1969 season.

And that's not all. In 1968, not only were both McLain and Gibson unanimous Cy Young winners, but both also were named Most Valuable Player in their respective leagues. McLain garnered a unanimous MVP vote, while Gibson outpointed the Cincinnati Reds' Pete Rose by 242–205.

Few right-handed pitchers intimidated a hitter the way Bob Gibson did. He threw his powerful fastball and devastating slider with an exaggerated, dramatic motion that carried him off the mound toward the first-base side.

"Gibson was maturing," said Cardinals third baseman Mike Shannon. "He was at his peak. I almost got a sore arm that year from throwing the ball around the infield after he'd strike people out."

"Hoot," as Gibson was sometimes called, fanned a league-leading 268, threw a league-best 13 shutouts, and held hitters to an incredibly low .184 average.

McLain used his lively fastball, a hard curve, and his brash demeanor to mow down AL batters. In 1968 he sported a 16–2 record at the All-Star break and never let up, finishing with a 31–6 mark. He also led the league with 28 complete games and 336 innings. He was second with 280 strikeouts and fourth with a 1.96 ERA, and he limited batters to a .200 average.

Left: McLain is the only 30-game winner in the past six decades. Here he shows his winning form in Game Six of the 1968 World Series. Opposite: Bob Gibson's suspended right leg is about to fall toward the first-base side of the mound as he completes his unique delivery during Game Four of the 1967 World Series. The Cards beat the Boston Red Sox in 7 games.

Detroit Tigers pitcher Denny McLain gets a hug from Al Kaline as they watch Willie Horton bring in Mickey Stanley for the decisive run of a September 14 game against visiting Oakland. The 5–4 victory was McLain's thirteenth win of the season.

DENNY McCLAIN

1968 AL WINNING STATS

WINS	31
LOSSES	6
PCT.	.838
ERA	1.96
GAMES	41
INNINGS	336
HITS	241
BASE ON BALLS	63
STRIKEOUTS	280
SHUTOUTS	6

1969 AL WINNING STATS (TIE)

WINS	24
LOSSES	9
PCT.	.727
ERA	2.80
GAMES	42
INNINGS	325
HITS	288
BASE ON BALLS	67
STRIKEOUTS	181
SHUTOUTS	9

"Denny McLain was a real student of pitching and the game," said Tigers pitching coach Johnny Sain, the legendary former Boston Braves pitcher who was himself a four-time 20-game winner.

That Gibson and McLain faced each other twice in the 1968 World Series seemed inevitable, but the matchups didn't live up to their advance billing. By the time the Series started, McLain fell victim to tendinitis in his throwing elbow. Gibson, meanwhile, was as dominating as ever. He beat McLain and the Tigers in Game One, 4–0 on a 5-hitter, while eclipsing Sandy Koufax's single-game strikeout mark with 17. The record still stands.

In Game Four, they met again with similar results. The Cardinals won, 10–1, as Gibson pitched another complete-game 5-hitter. He struck out ten and hit a home run. McLain was replaced in the third inning.

The Cardinals eventually took a 3–1 lead in the Series and seemed ready to repeat as champions, but after a 3-run first inning in Game Five, the Cards were shut out by Mickey Lolich, setting up Game Six.

BOB GIBSON

1968 NL WINNING STATS

WINS	21
LOSSES	9
PCT.	.710
ERA	1.12
GAMES	34
INNINGS	304.2
HITS	198
BASE ON BALLS	62
STRIKEOUTS	268
SHUTOUTS	13

1970 NL WINNING STATS

WINS	23
LOSSES	7
PCT.	.767
ERA	3.12
GAMES	34
INNINGS	294
HITS	262
BASE ON BALLS	88
STRIKEOUTS	274
SHUTOUTS	3

Finally, McLain delivered. He pitched Detroit into Game Seven by scattering 9 hits in the Tigers' 13–1 win. The stage was set for Gibson to nail down the trophy for St. Louis, but Lolich, another 2-game winner, was standing in his way.

And it was Lolich who pulled off the upset, earning his third win and a World Series MVP Award, as the Tigers won 4–1 to take the Series. Gibson could only console himself with the fact that his 35 strikeouts set a single Series record.

In 1969, McLain became only the second pitcher to win the Cy Young Award more than once, joining three-time winner Sandy Koufax. Denny, who was tied in the voting with Baltimore's Mike Cuellar, led the league with 24 wins, 9 shutouts, and 325 innings.

Gibson won his second Cy Young Award in 1970, when he led the league with 23 wins against only 7 losses, and struck out 274 in 294 innings. When he finished his seventeen-year career—all with St. Louis—he had totaled 251 wins, nine 200-plus strikeout seasons, a lifetime 2.91 ERA, and 3,117 strikeouts (tenth on the all-time list).

After striking out a record seventeen Tigers in Game One of the 1968 World Series, Bob Gibson gets a pat on the back from catcher Tim McCarver and a handshake from first baseman Orlando Cepeda.

Pitching for Cleveland in 1972, Perry had a slider that was a constant source of frustration for AL hitters in his first Cy Young season.

GAYLORD PERRY

Gaylord Perry began his twenty-two-year career in 1962 with the NL champion San Francisco Giants. In his ten-year stint in the Bay Area, he was a 20-game winner twice, once with a league-leading 23 wins in 1970.

Perry's first Cy Young Award came in 1972 in the American League while on the mound for the fifth-place Cleveland Indians. (This was two years after his older brother Jim received the Cy Young when pitching for the Minnesota Twins. Jim and Gaylord constitute the only brother act to have grabbed Cy Young honors.) That year he fashioned a 1.92 ERA and won a league-best 24 games—one-third of the Tribe's total victories.

His second Cy Young honor came in 1978, when he was a member of the San Diego Padres. Back in the National League after six years with Cleveland and the Texas Rangers, Perry logged a 21–6 record, leading the league in wins and win-

1972 NL WINNING STATS

WINS	24
LOSSES	16
PCT.	.600
ERA	1.92
GAMES	41
INNINGS	343
HITS	253
BASE ON BALLS	82
STRIKEOUTS	234
SHUTOUTS	5

1978 NL WINNING STATS

WINS	21
LOSSES	6
PCT.	.778
ERA	2.72
GAMES	37
INNINGS	261
HITS	241
BASE ON BALLS	66
STRIKEOUTS	154
SHUTOUTS	2

Look, Ma, no grease. No, Gaylord Perry isn't baring his head for a pop inspection. He is doffing his cap to appreciative fans in Seattle after winning his 300th game in 1982, in which he beat the New York Yankees, 7–4.

Gaylord the Cheater

Although he admitted that he sometimes cheated, that doesn't mean that Gaylord Perry relied on doctoring the ball for all of his 314 wins. You've got to have some stuff in order to win two Cy Young Awards and make it into the Hall of Fame.

In his book, *Me and the Spitter*, Perry caused a stir late in the 1973 season by admitting that he used foreign substances to alter the path of his pitches. This was no big surprise to many players and managers, who had been watching his pitching routine for years: the tugging of the sleeve, the pitching hand always somewhere around his head before a pitch.

But Perry performed well under his critics' acute scrutiny the following year, winning 21 games while pitching for fourth-place Cleveland. "He had a great sinker," said Indians catcher Dave Duncan, a defender of Perry who claims that the pitcher threw only one spitter a year. "He just kept up the act to make hitters believe he was loading up the ball. So they focused on trying to catch him cheating instead of concentrating on how he was pitching them."

Indeed, New York Yankee Bobby Murcer was fined $250 in 1973 for saying that Commissioner Bowie Kuhn was "gutless" for not suspending Perry. Gaylord took the incident in stride. "Bobby was just saying that after a loss in the excitement. I like him. He's just trying to win. So am I."

Gaylord Perry, shown here playing for the San Diego Padres in the early eighties, was the master of deceptive pitches.

ning percentage. With this second Cy Young, Gaylord became the only pitcher to have won the award in each league; he retains the honor to this day. He finished his career ranked sixth on the all-time strikeout list with 3,534 and fourteenth in wins with 314.

Perry's trademark pitch was his hard slider, which broke down and away from right-handed hitters—a motion so drastic it prompted continual cries from hitters and managers who swore Perry was throwing a spitball. Though he denied such charges throughout his career, after his retirement, Perry finally admitted to using a spitball. The admission probably cost him a first-ballot entry into the Hall of Fame, but Perry is enshrined in Cooperstown nonetheless.

BRET SABERHAGEN

Bret Saberhagen was the youngest pitcher ever to win the Cy Young Award in the American League. In 1985, at the age of twenty-one, he won his first Cy Young Award while pitching for the Kansas City Royals. His encore season came in 1989—when he was already a seasoned four-year veteran.

Opposite: Though Bret Saberhagen began his career with Kansas City, he now pitches for the New York Mets. Big Apple fans are hoping that "Sabes" can follow in Gaylord Perry's footsteps by winning Cy Young Awards in both leagues. Above: When he is healthy, Saberhagen is tough to get a hit off of.

What a storybook year 1985 was for Bret Saberhagen. In only his second year in the big leagues, pitching for the Kansas City Royals, "Sabes" went 20–6 with a 2.87 ERA while walking only 1.5 batters per game. He outpolled 22 game–winner Ron Guidry in the Cy Young voting that year, 127–88. Saberhagen then capped off the year by earning World Series MVP honors as he helped pitch his Royals to the World Championship over St. Louis.

All at the tender age of twenty-one.

Unfortunately, Bret's body proved tender, too. Injury in 1986 proved his undoing as he slid all the way to a 7–12 record. He rebounded to 18–10 in 1987, but slid once more to a disappointing 14–16 record in 1988.

In 1989, however, a healthier and wiser Saberhagen rebounded with a sterling 23–6 record to lead the league in wins and with his 2.16 ERA.

"I had trouble winning regularly after 1985," Saberhagen told reporters after winning his second Cy Young Award, "because of injuries and because of not knowing how to keep winning. But I learned. Toward the end of this season, I was throwing as good as I can throw."

1985 AL WINNING STATS

WINS	20
LOSSES	6
PCT.	.769
ERA	2.87
GAMES	32
INNINGS	235.1
HITS	211
BASE ON BALLS	38
STRIKEOUTS	158
SHUTOUTS	1

1989 AL WINNING STATS

WINS	23
LOSSES	6
PCT.	.793
ERA	2.16
GAMES	36
INNINGS	262.1
HITS	209
BASE ON BALLS	43
STRIKEOUTS	193
SHUTOUTS	4

Sabes' Comeback

The only problem with being so successful at such a young age is that everybody expects you to be able to do it all over again the next year.

Unfortunately for Bret Saberhagen, his celebration party after his triumphant 1985 season lasted so long that he suffered from a bad hangover for the entire 1986 season.

"I hurt in so many places that I felt thirty-seven," said the 1985 Cy Young Award winner and World Series MVP, who was all of twenty-one when he arrived at spring training in 1986. That spring heralded a dismal season in which he plummeted from a 20–6 record and postseason glory to 7–12 and a 4.15 ERA.

Looking back in June 1987, Saberhagen was able to put things in a clearer perspective. "I had no way to answer the people who thought it had all gone to—or through—my head. I'm the same person now that I was last year, and in '85."

At the time those comments were made, Sabes could afford to be more optimistic. After an effective off-season training routine that allowed him to work out nagging injuries to his arm and foot, Saberhagen got off to a 9–1 start, with a 2.33 ERA. And as early as June, he had already had 2 starts in which he kept batters at bay into the seventh inning, and was also getting more pop on his fastball that he had had all the previous year.

"A big part of his success," explained catcher Jamie Quirk in 1987, "comes from his confidence, and he lost it last year. It's back. He hasn't just come back. He has come back better."

It hadn't taken Bret long to figure out that hard work was the key. "I looked in the mirror and knew that when I got to spring training in '86, I wasn't prepared. I found out I could no longer just walk in and win."

But it was fun while it lasted: personal appearances, including a spot on *The Tonight Show*, adoring fans, and a raise from $100,000 to $925,000. "I learned the hard way," Saberhagen said. "I didn't get any rest, mentally or physically."

So for 1986, he did not live up to the standards he set the previous year, but in 1987 he certainly made amends, winning 18 of the 33 games he pitched.

Onetime Wonders: Starters and Relievers

While players like Steve Carlton, Sandy Koufax, and Tom Seaver have dominated the Cy Young stage, there have been many pitchers over the years who have produced one brilliant season and won the award. However, baseball fans in New York City have had more than their share of onetime wonders.

Don Newcombe, Whitey Ford, Ron Guidry, and Dwight Gooden were all New York starting pitchers who had career years to win their one and only Cy Young Award in each of four consecutive decades.

Will the nineties produce a fifth? If so, the next Big Apple Cy Young soloist might be another starter, though chances are better he would be a reliever.

STARTERS

For many years the words "pitcher" and "starter" were synonymous. Although nowadays there are clearly two types of pitchers, the starting pitcher is still the central figure on the diamond. Most times it is he who is credited with a team's win or loss. Thus, starting pitchers have monopolized the Cy Young voting.

DON NEWCOMBE—1956

"Newk" helped pitch the defending world champion Brooklyn Dodgers back into the World Series in 1956 with a .794 winning percentage and a league-low .221 batting average against him. He also ranked second in the league in fewest hits per game, fewest walks per game, and most shutouts. Unfortunately for the Dodgers, Newk couldn't maintain his Cy Young form in the 1956 World Series, where he was bombed by the Yankees in Games Two and Seven.

1956 NL WINNING STATS	
WINS	27
LOSSES	7
PCT.	.794
ERA	3.06
GAMES	38
INNINGS	268
HITS	219
BASE ON BALLS	46
STRIKEOUTS	139
SHUTOUTS	5

A Winning Combination: Cy Young Award and MVP Award

••••••••••••••••••••••••••••••

Wouldn't you just know it? As soon as baseball gets around to giving pitchers their own award to distinguish their accomplishments in their own specialized craft, the first Cy Young Award winner also wins the Most Valuable Player Award.

Brooklyn's Don Newcombe, who went 27–7 in 1956, captured both awards to lead the defending world champion Dodgers back to the World Series.

So much for the argument that a pitcher shouldn't win the MVP because he's not an "everyday player." Although this debate picked up momentum after the institution of the Cy Young Award, it did not stop nine pitchers from winning both awards in the same season.

When the anemic-hitting Los Angeles Dodgers won the NL pennant in 1963, Sandy Koufax and his 25 wins got much of the credit. So did Bob Gibson (22–9) of the St. Louis Cardinals (National League) and Denny McLain (31–6) of the Detroit Tigers (American League) for their respective pennant victories in 1968.

Two other dominating starters, Vida Blue and Roger Clemens, also pitched their teams to division titles. Blue (24–8, 1.82 ERA) did it with Oakland in 1971, while Clemens (24–4, 2.48 ERA) imposed his will on AL batters in 1986 while pitching for the Boston Red Sox.

With the full flowering of the relief pitcher as dominating specialist in the colorful 1970s, three pitchers have since delighted in the distinctive double: Rollie Fingers, Milwaukee Brewers, 1981 (28 saves, 1.04 ERA); Willie Hernandez, Detroit Tigers, 1984 (32 saves, 1.93 ERA); and Dennis Eckersley, Oakland A's, 1992 (51 saves, 1.91 ERA).

WARREN SPAHN—1957

Most of his career 363 wins—a record for left-handers—came prior to the Cy Young Award's inception, but "Spahnie" made up for lost time in the Milwaukee Braves' 1957 world championship season. The screwballing Hall of Famer led the league with 21 wins and 18 complete games, and posted a 2.69 ERA.

Don Newcombe stretches his large frame as he delivers another pitch for the Brooklyn Dodgers in 1955.

1957 NL WINNING STATS

WINS	21
LOSSES	11
PCT.	.656
ERA	2.69
GAMES	39
INNINGS	271
HITS	241
BASE ON BALLS	78
STRIKEOUTS	111
SHUTOUTS	4

EARLY WYNN—1959

A four-time 20-game winner earlier in his Hall of Fame career with the Cleveland Indians, Wynn led the American League with 22 wins for the World Series–bound Chicago White Sox. The career 300-game winner limited batters to a .216 average and twirled a league-high 256 innings.

VERNON LAW—1960

In 1960 Law won 20 games during the regular season and the Pittsburgh Pirates won their first pennant since 1927. Law added 2 wins in Pittsburgh's World Series victory over the Yankees, giving the Pirates their first Series title since 1925.

BOB TURLEY—1958

"Bullet Bob" scorched his way through AL bats, allowing a league-low .206 batting average and 6.5 hits per game. He also led the league with 21 wins and 19 complete games, helping the New York Yankees to a world championship.

1958 AL WINNING STATS	
WINS	21
LOSSES	7
PCT.	.750
ERA	2.97
GAMES	33
INNINGS	245.1
HITS	178
BASE ON BALLS	128
STRIKEOUTS	168
SHUTOUTS	6

1959 AL WINNING STATS	
WINS	22
LOSSES	10
PCT.	.688
ERA	3.17
GAMES	37
INNINGS	255.2
HITS	202
BASE ON BALLS	119
STRIKEOUTS	179
SHUTOUTS	5

1960 NL WINNING STATS	
WINS	20
LOSSES	9
PCT.	.690
ERA	3.08
GAMES	35
INNINGS	271.2
HITS	266
BASE ON BALLS	40
STRIKEOUTS	120
SHUTOUTS	3

WHITEY FORD—1961

The single most distinguishing characteristic of Whitey Ford's career was his consistency. His .690 career winning percentage still stands as the all-time best. He won 236 games in his Hall of Fame career to complement his sparkling 2.74 earned run average. When the "Chairman of the Board" took the mound, he took charge in a businesslike way, methodically working his way through a line-up. Anytime the wily left-hander pitched, odds were in the Yankees' favor.

Ford reeled off thirteen straight seasons of double-digit wins, including ten seasons in which he won at least 16 games. The highlight of his career came in 1961, when he won a career-best 25 games against only 4 losses for an .862 winning percentage. During that remarkable season, Whitey got relief help from Luis Arroyo, who saved 29 games and himself won 15, and plenty of run support from a devastating crew that was a latter-day version of the Yankees' 1927 "Murderers' Row." Led by Roger Maris' record 61 homers and Mickey Mantle's career-high 54 blasts, the Yankees set a major league mark that year with 240 home runs.

Ford shut out the Cincinnati Reds in Game One of the 1961 World Series, and then went on to set a World Series record in Game Four by pitching 5 more consecutive scoreless innings to push his streak to 32, passing Babe Ruth's previous record of 29⅔ innings.

1961 AL WINNING STATS

WINS	25
LOSSES	4
PCT.	.862
ERA	3.21
GAMES	39
INNINGS	283
HITS	242
BASE ON BALLS	92
STRIKEOUTS	209
SHUTOUTS	3

Don Drysdale—1962

Although often overshadowed by his Los Angeles Dodgers teammate Sandy Koufax, Don Drysdale still had an imposing presence from the right side of the mound. His six feet five inches were coupled with a powerful inside fastball that translated into a league-leading 25 wins, 314 innings, and 232 strikeouts for the Hall of Famer.

Dean Chance—1964

Using pinpoint control that resulted in just 86 walks in a league-leading 278 innings, Chance led the majors with a 1.65 ERA and 11 shutouts. He also led the American League with 15 complete games and tied for the league lead with 20 wins, a remarkable feat considering his Los Angeles Angels finished just barely above .500.

Mike McCormick—NL 1967

In the first year of dual-league balloting, McCormick led his league with 22 wins and was second with 5 shutouts. The six-foot-two-inch San Francisco Giant had a 2.85 ERA.

1962 NL WINNING STATS	
WINS	25
LOSSES	9
PCT.	.735
ERA	2.83
GAMES	43
INNINGS	314.1
HITS	272
BASE ON BALLS	78
STRIKEOUTS	232
SHUTOUTS	2

1964 NL WINNING STATS	
WINS	20
LOSSES	9
PCT.	.690
ERA	1.65
GAMES	46
INNINGS	278.1
HITS	194
BASE ON BALLS	86
STRIKEOUTS	207
SHUTOUTS	11

1967 NL WINNING STATS	
WINS	22
LOSSES	10
PCT.	.688
ERA	2.85
GAMES	40
INNINGS	262.1
HITS	220
BASE ON BALLS	81
STRIKEOUTS	150
SHUTOUTS	5

JIM LONBORG—AL 1967

Jim posted a league-high 22 wins and 246 strike-outs. The six-foot-five-inch Lonborg held batters to a .225 average and topped off his stellar season by winning 2 of the 3 games he pitched in the World Series. Ultimately, however, the Red Sox lost in the final game.

MIKE CUELLAR—AL 1969

Cuellar tied with Detroit's two-time winner Denny McLain in the voting, the only tie in the Cy Young Award's history. The Orioles' lefty screwballer won 23 games, allowed a meager .204 batting average, and had a 2.38 ERA for the AL champions.

1969 AL WINNING STATS (TIE)	
WINS	23
LOSSES	11
PCT.	.676
ERA	2.38
GAMES	39
INNINGS	290.2
HITS	213
BASE ON BALLS	79
STRIKEOUTS	182
SHUTOUTS	5

1967 AL WINNING STATS	
WINS	22
LOSSES	9
PCT.	.710
ERA	3.16
GAMES	39
INNINGS	273.1
HITS	228
BASE ON BALLS	83
STRIKEOUTS	246
SHUTOUTS	2

JIM PERRY—AL 1970

One half of the only Cy Young brother act (younger brother Gaylord was a two-time winner), Jim led the American League in 1970 with 24 wins as the Twins took the Western Division title. Walking a mere fifty-seven batters in 279 innings, Perry hurled 13 complete games and recorded a 3.03 ERA.

FERGUSON JENKINS—NL 1971

Give the six-foot-five-inch Hall of Famer an A-plus for control. "Fergie" dished out only 37 free passes while pitching a league-leading 325 innings. He led the league with 24 wins and 30 complete games, and had a tidy 2.77 ERA. However, the Chicago Cubs were unable to finish higher than third in the NL West.

VIDA BLUE—AL 1971

Vida helped pitch the Oakland A's into the play-offs while making AL hitters blue. He led the league with 24 wins, 8 shutouts, and a 1.82 ERA, and held batters to a stingy .189 average. His 301 strikeouts were a close AL second to Mickey Lolich's 308 for the Detroit Tigers.

1970 AL WINNING STATS	
WINS	24
LOSSES	12
PCT.	.667
ERA	3.03
GAMES	40
INNINGS	279
HITS	258
BASE ON BALLS	57
STRIKEOUTS	168
SHUTOUTS	4

1971 NL WINNING STATS	
WINS	24
LOSSES	13
PCT.	.649
ERA	2.77
GAMES	39
INNINGS	325
HITS	304
BASE ON BALLS	37
STRIKEOUTS	263
SHUTOUTS	3

1971 AL WINNING STATS	
WINS	24
LOSSES	8
PCT.	.750
ERA	1.82
GAMES	39
INNINGS	312
HITS	209
BASE ON BALLS	88
STRIKEOUTS	301
SHUTOUTS	8

Randy Jones—NL 1976

Of the three dozen or so pitchers named Jones in major league history, only Randall Leo Jones can lay claim to a Cy Young Award. He proved that his 20 wins in 1975 were no fluke when a year later he led the National League with 22 wins. The San Diego Padres may have won only 73 games that year, but Jones still maintained a 2.74 ERA and led the league with 25 complete games and 315 innings.

1976 NL WINNING STATS	
WINS	22
LOSSES	14
PCT.	.611
ERA	2.74
GAMES	40
INNINGS	315.1
HITS	274
BASE ON BALLS	50
STRIKEOUTS	93
SHUTOUTS	5

Jim Hunter—AL 1974

"Catfish" was the most celebrated money pitcher of his day. This Hall of Famer won 4 career play-off games and added another 5 victories in World Series play for the A's and later for the New York Yankees. In 1974, he led the league with 25 wins and a 2.49 ERA, while helping to pitch Oakland to its third straight World Series victory.

1974 AL WINNING STATS	
WINS	25
LOSSES	12
PCT.	.676
ERA	2.49
GAMES	41
INNINGS	318
HITS	268
BASE ON BALLS	46
STRIKEOUTS	143
SHUTOUTS	6

RON GUIDRY—AL 1978

In 1978, Ron Guidry conjured echoes of Whitey Ford's memorable 1961 season with his own incredible season to remember. In earning a rare unanimous Cy Young vote, the "Louisiana Lightnin'" carved out a glittering 25–3 record with a miniscule 1.74 ERA. (The next-best ERA in the entire major leagues was 2.27.) Guidry allowed a major league–low 6.14 hits per game and a league-best .193 batting average, and ranked second in the league with 248 strikeouts.

Guidry pitched the New York Yankees back into the World Series by outdueling Dennis Leonard of the Kansas City Royals, 2–1 (with relief help from Goose Gossage), in Game Four of the AL playoffs to clinch the Series. He also won Game Three of the World Series, which the Yanks eventually won in 6 games.

"Gid" came close to winning a second Cy Young Award in 1985, when he went 22–6 with a 3.27 ERA, but finished second to Kansas City's Bret Saberhagen in the voting.

1978 AL WINNING STATS

WINS	25
LOSSES	3
PCT.	.893
ERA	1.74
GAMES	35
INNINGS	273.2
HITS	187
BASE ON BALLS	72
STRIKEOUTS	248
SHUTOUTS	9

STEVE STONE—AL 1980

Stone's league-leading 25 wins helped the Orioles place back-to-back Cy Young soloists. "Stoney" lost just 7 games, to lead the league with a .781 winning percentage.

MIKE FLANAGAN—AL 1979

Flanagan's league-leading 23 wins were a big reason the Orioles won both the Eastern Division and the AL playoffs. He also led the league that year with 5 shutouts.

FERNANDO VALENZUELA—NL 1981

The left-handed, screwballing phenomenon astounded the baseball world with 8 straight wins, including 5 shutouts, to open the strike-shortened season. He finished at 13–7 and led the league with 11 complete games, 8 shutouts, 192 innings, and 180 strikeouts. He also picked up 3 postseason wins for the world champion Dodgers, including Game Three of the World Series against the Yankees. And as if that weren't enough, he won the Rookie of the Year Award.

1980 AL WINNING STATS

WINS	25
LOSSES	7
PCT.	.781
ERA	3.23
GAMES	37
INNINGS	251
HITS	224
BASE ON BALLS	101
STRIKEOUTS	149
SHUTOUTS	1

1979 AL WINNING STATS

WINS	23
LOSSES	9
PCT.	.719
ERA	3.08
GAMES	39
INNINGS	266
HITS	245
BASE ON BALLS	70
STRIKEOUTS	190
SHUTOUTS	5

1981 NL WINNING STATS

WINS	13
LOSSES	7
PCT.	.650
ERA	2.48
GAMES	25
INNINGS	192
HITS	140
BASE ON BALLS	61
STRIKEOUTS	180
SHUTOUTS	8

PETE VUCKOVICH—AL 1982

Vuckovich won 93 games in his eleven-year major league career, and 18 of those came in a year highlighted by the Milwaukee Brewer's appearance in the 1982 World Series. His 18–6 mark constituted a .750 winning percentage, the best in the league.

JOHN DENNY—NL 1983

John went 19–6 for a league-leading .760 winning percentage, and the Phillies went to the World Series. He had a 2.37 ERA during the regular season and helped the Phillies to their only win in the Fall Classic.

LAMARR HOYT—AL 1983

The big right-hander led the AL with 24 wins and walked a minuscule 31 batters in 261 innings. Although he had a somewhat inflated 3.66 ERA, he led the league in limiting opponents' on-base average to .259. Hoyt outdueled Baltimore's Scott McGregor, 2–1, in Game One of the American League playoffs, although the Orioles went on to beat the White Sox in the next 3 games and advance to the World Series.

1982 AL WINNING STATS	
WINS	18
LOSSES	6
PCT.	.750
ERA	3.34
GAMES	30
INNINGS	223.2
HITS	234
BASE ON BALLS	102
STRIKEOUTS	105
SHUTOUTS	1

1983 NL WINNING STATS	
WINS	19
LOSSES	6
PCT.	.760
ERA	2.37
GAMES	36
INNINGS	242.2
HITS	229
BASE ON BALLS	53
STRIKEOUTS	139
SHUTOUTS	1

1983 AL WINNING STATS	
WINS	24
LOSSES	10
PCT.	.706
ERA	3.66
GAMES	36
INNINGS	260.2
HITS	236
BASE ON BALLS	31
STRIKEOUTS	148
SHUTOUTS	1

RICK SUTCLIFFE—NL 1984

The "Red Baron" enjoyed a new lease on life when the Cleveland Indians traded him to Chicago in the early days of the 1984 season. While with the Eastern Division champion Cubs, Sutcliffe logged an astonishing 16–1 record, a 2.70 ERA, and 155 strikeouts in 150 innings. His record with the Cubbies, coupled with his earlier 4 wins in the American League, made him a 20-game winner for the season.

1984 NL WINNING STATS

WINS	16
LOSSES	1
PCT.	.941
ERA	2.70
GAMES	20
INNINGS	150
HITS	123
BASE ON BALLS	39
STRIKEOUTS	155
SHUTOUTS	3

DWIGHT GOODEN—NL 1985

In 1985, the New York Mets' Dwight Gooden was single-handedly rekindling memories of Bob Gibson's 1968 campaign. "Doctor K" earned his nickname in 1984 when, at the tender age of nineteen, he set a rookie record with 276 strikeouts and won the Rookie of the Year Award. He added another 268 whiffs in his sophomore season, giving him a major league–record 544—the most strikeouts ever in a pitcher's first two seasons.

Doc became the first pitcher since the incomparable Sandy Koufax to lead the majors in pitching's Triple Crown: a season's most wins, most strikeouts, and lowest ERA. He went 24–4, including 14 straight wins, and pitched 8 shutouts while recording a stingy 1.53 ERA, the lowest in the majors since Gibson's 1.12 in 1968. Gooden also led the league with 277 innings and 16 complete games, and ranked second with an .857 winning percentage and a .201 average allowed against him.

In earning unanimous acclaim, Gooden, at age twenty, became the youngest Cy Young Award winner in baseball history.

1985 NL WINNING STATS

WINS	24
LOSSES	4
PCT.	.857
ERA	1.53
GAMES	35
INNINGS	276.2
HITS	198
BASE ON BALLS	69
STRIKEOUTS	268
SHUTOUTS	8

OREL HERSHISER—NL 1988

In 1988, Orel Hershiser performed surgery on NL hitters, limiting them to a .213 average while fashioning a 2.26 ERA. Hershiser threw 59 consecutive scoreless innings, breaking the twenty-year-old record of 58 held by another Dodger, Don Drysdale. He also won the MVP Awards for both the NL playoffs and the World Series. The lanky hurler used a devastating slider and impeccable control to lead the league with 23 wins, 15 complete games, 8 shutouts, and 267 innings.

MIKE SCOTT—NL 1986

Houston's Mike Scott became the first pitcher to clinch a division title by throwing a no-hitter. He used a live fastball with an unhittable split-fingered speeder as a devastating one-two punch, holding batters to a league-low .186 average. The righty also led the league with 306 strikeouts, 275 innings, a 2.22 ERA, 5 shutouts, and 6 hits per game. Scott beat the eventual world champion New York Mets twice in the NL playoffs to earn MVP honors in a losing cause.

1986 NL WINNING STATS	
WINS	18
LOSSES	10
PCT.	.643
ERA	2.22
GAMES	37
INNINGS	275.1
HITS	182
BASE ON BALLS	72
STRIKEOUTS	306
SHUTOUTS	5

1988 NL WINNING STATS	
WINS	23
LOSSES	8
PCT.	.742
ERA	2.26
GAMES	35
INNINGS	267
HITS	208
BASE ON BALLS	73
STRIKEOUTS	178
SHUTOUTS	8

DOUG DRABEK—NL 1990

A strong finisher, Drabek led the league with 22 wins and a .786 winning percentage, having lost only 6 games. The crafty right-hander walked 56 in 231 innings, fashioned a 2.76 ERA, and was second in the league with 9 complete games for the Eastern Division champion Pirates.

1990 NL WINNING STATS	
WINS	22
LOSSES	6
PCT.	.786
ERA	2.76
GAMES	33
INNINGS	231.1
HITS	190
BASE ON BALLS	56
STRIKEOUTS	131
SHUTOUTS	3

FRANK VIOLA—AL 1988

The tall left-hander, master of the "circle change," had AL hitters lunging for his off-speed stuff and watching his crisp fastball go by. Making a circle with his thumb and index finger to throw his unhittable change-up, "Frankie V" sailed to a 24–7 record with a 2.64 ERA. The Twins, however, were unable to repeat the previous year's fabulous performance and finished second in the AL West.

1988 AL WINNING STATS	
WINS	24
LOSSES	7
PCT.	.774
ERA	2.64
GAMES	35
INNINGS	255.1
HITS	236
BASE ON BALLS	54
STRIKEOUTS	193
SHUTOUTS	2

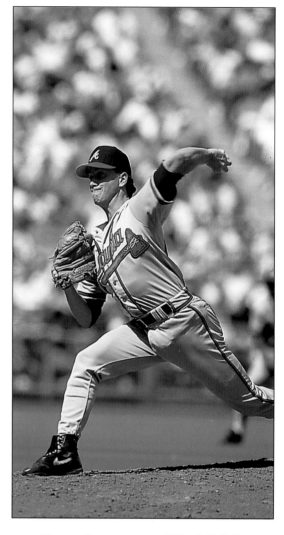

TOM GLAVINE—NL 1991

Another crafty lefty with a great change-up and pinpoint control, Glavine went 20–11 with a 2.55 ERA and 192 strikeouts. He also outpitched Minnesota Twin Kevin Tapani to win Game Five of the World Series. The Braves, however, lost the next 2 games and the Series.

BOB WELCH—AL 1990

Welch's 27 wins were the highest in the majors since 1972. Losing only 6 games, he led the league with an .818 winning percentage. He won Game Two of the AL playoffs against the Boston Red Sox and helped pitch the defending world champion A's back into the World Series.

1990 AL WINNING STATS	
WINS	27
LOSSES	6
PCT.	.818
ERA	2.95
GAMES	35
INNINGS	238
HITS	214
BASE ON BALLS	77
STRIKEOUTS	127
SHUTOUTS	2

1991 NL WINNING STATS	
WINS	20
LOSSES	11
PCT.	.645
ERA	2.55
GAMES	34
INNINGS	246.2
HITS	201
BASE ON BALLS	69
STRIKEOUTS	192
SHUTOUTS	1

RANDY JOHNSON—AL 1995

The "Big Unit" came up a big winner for the Seattle Mariners as the team advanced to the postseason for the first time in its nineteen-year history.

Always known as a strikeout pitcher with a near-100-mph fastball, Johnson led the major leagues for the fourth straight year with 294 whiffs. He became the first Seattle player to win a postseason award.

"My teammates now come up and ask me when I'm pitching, instead of asking when I'm throwing," said Johnson after hearing of his victory in the Cy Young voting. He garnered twenty-six of a possible twenty-eight first place votes for 136 points, well ahead of Cleveland's Jose Mesa, who earned the remaining first-place votes and fifty-four points.

DAVID CONE—AL 1994

Kansas City's Coneheads were out in full force to celebrate David's 16–5 1994 season. His win total was just one shy of the AL lead in the strike-abbreviated season, and his 2.94 ERA was third-best for the year.

The wiry right-hander used his blazing fastball, hard slider, and sidearm curve to hold opponents to an average of 6.82 hits per game, second-best in the league.

The award was particularly satisfying for "Coney," who finished a distant third to Orel Hershiser in 1988, despite logging an outstanding 20–3 record for the New York Mets that year.

JACK McDOWELL—AL 1993

Through the 1993 season, "Black Jack" had 73 wins in the nineties, more than any pitcher for the decade. He finished second in the Cy Young balloting in 1992 and finally got over the hump in 1993 with a league-leading 22 wins and 4 shutouts for the Western Division champion White Sox.

1993 AL WINNING STATS	
WINS	22
LOSSES	10
PCT.	.688
ERA	3.37
GAMES	34
INNINGS	256.2
HITS	261
BASE ON BALLS	69
STRIKEOUTS	158
SHUTOUTS	4

1994 AL WINNING STATS	
WINS	16
LOSSES	5
PCT.	.762
ERA	2.94
GAMES	23
INNINGS	171.6
HITS	130
BASE ON BALLS	54
STRIKEOUTS	132
SHUTOUTS	3

1995 AL WINNING STATS	
WINS	18
LOSSES	2
PCT.	.900
ERA	2.48
GAMES	30
INNINGS	214.1
HITS	159
BASE ON BALLS	65
STRIKEOUTS	294
SHUTOUTS	3

A relief specialist in the vein of Joe Page of the Yankees, Jim Konstanty of Philadelphia was part of a rare breed in the 1940s and '50s. It wasn't until the 1970s that relief pitchers, as we know them today, became abundant.

RELIEVERS

Since the early 1970s, the role of the bullpen has changed. Today, relief pitchers are specialists, called upon to dominate an opposing lineup in the late innings, protect a lead, and save a win. Many great relievers have emerged over the past two decades, thus writing a new chapter in the history of pitching.

Before the seventies, most relievers were ex–starting pitchers who had lost their effectiveness over a 6- or 7-inning performance. A manager's last resort before sending a starter to the minors was to put him in the pen, hoping the hurler could at least pitch an effective inning or two and maybe regain his old form and return to the rotation.

But as always with general rules of thumb, there were exceptions.

In 1950, Jim Konstanty of the Philadelphia Phillies was a dominant relief pitcher despite being thirty-three years old. One of the few "Whiz Kids" over the age of twenty-five, the right-hander emerged from the bullpen seventy-four times to win 16 games, lose only 7, and save 22. He pitched 152 innings, all in relief, and claimed a 2.66 ERA while holding opponents to a .205 batting average.

That season, he helped pitch the youthful Phillies into the World Series while also earning himself the National League's Most Valuable Player Award—six years before the Cy Young Award was created. Ironically, when the World Series rolled around, Konstanty was tabbed as a starter for the first time all season. Not surprisingly, though, he pitched very well in Game One, allowing only 1 run in 8 innings. But he lost, 1–0, to Vic Raschi and the New York Yankees.

Until 1970, only one reliever—Lindy McDaniel of the St. Louis Cardinals—received any Cy Young votes, and he got only one. In 1970, however, Dave Giusti of Houston and Minnesota Twin Ron Perranoski did receive votes—eight and five, respectively.

The turning point for relievers came in the 1972 World Series, in which Cincinnati Reds manager Sparky Anderson earned the nickname "Captain Hook" for his liberal use of bullpen pitchers. Sparky reasoned that there was no sense in using his starters for 7 or 8 innings when he had four or five fresh arms in the bullpen who could enter the game and throw as hard as the starters had.

Sparky reasoned that it was tougher on the hitters in the late innings to see a new pitcher with new stuff, as opposed to facing the starting pitcher for a third or fourth time. The theory was widely questioned at first, of course, as are most new ideas in baseball. Anderson, however, had already utilized this practice during the regular season, and top Reds reliever Clay Carroll saved 37 games that year, then a major league record.

Additional proof came during that 1972 Series as the Reds erased a 3–1 game deficit to force a Game Seven, which the A's won by the closest of margins, 3–2.

In those games in which Anderson went to his bullpen as early as the sixth inning—Games Two, Five, Six, and Seven—Oakland scored 4 or fewer runs. The Reds won Games Five and Six and lost Games Two and Seven by 1 run each.

Anderson used a bevy of relievers—Pedro Borbon, Tom Hall, and Carroll—and even starters Ross Grimsley and Jack Billingham. By the next year, even the Oakland A's caught on, using reliever Darold Knowles in a record 7 games.

Thus, a major trend in bullpen usage was born. Relievers have since become specialists in their own right and are no longer simply former starters relegated to the outer reaches of the stadium. Their legitimacy as a new and important part of the game took a giant step forward in 1974, when Mike Marshall of the NL champion Los Angeles Dodgers became the first reliever to win the Cy Young Award. Marshall appeared in a record 106 games, had a 15–12 record, saved a league-leading 21 games (he saved 31 the year before), and recorded a 2.42 ERA. In the years that followed, seven other relievers won the Cy Young Award.

SPARKY LYLE—AL 1977

A quick wit and a hard slider were this lefty's trademarks as he compiled a 13–5 record with 26 saves and a 2.17 ERA for the world champion New York Yankees.

1977 AL WINNING STATS

WINS	13
LOSSES	5
PCT.	.722
ERA	2.17
GAMES	72
INNINGS	137
HITS	131
BASE ON BALLS	33
STRIKEOUTS	68
SAVES	26

BRUCE SUTTER—NL 1979

Armed with an all but unhittable split-fingered fastball, Sutter allowed a downright greedy 67 hits in 101 innings. He led the National League with 37 saves, as dumbfounded batters scratched out a meager .186 average. The Cubs, unfortunately, barely won 50 percent.

1979 NL WINNING STATS

WINS	6
LOSSES	6
PCT.	.500
ERA	2.23
GAMES	62
INNINGS	101
HITS	67
BASE ON BALLS	32
STRIKEOUTS	110
SAVES	37

ROLLIE FINGERS—AL 1981

With wax on his mustache and mustard on his fastball, Fingers picked up a league-high 28 saves to go along with his microscopic 1.04 ERA. This Hall of Famer won 6 games and league MVP honors for the divisional champion Brewers in the strike-shortened season.

1981 AL WINNING STATS

WINS	6
LOSSES	3
PCT.	.667
ERA	1.04
GAMES	47
INNINGS	78
HITS	55
BASE ON BALLS	13
STRIKEOUTS	61
SAVES	28

STEVE BEDROSIAN—NL 1987

NL hitters found the batter's box a hard place to be when they faced "Bedrock," who led the league with 40 saves. The fifth-place Phillies won only 80 games in 1987, but Steve saved half of them. From 1986 to 1988, Bedrosian saved a total of 97 games for Philadelphia.

WILLIE HERNANDEZ—AL 1984

The left-handed closer deluxe not only won the Cy Young, but also snagged the MVP Award as he stifled AL hitters to the tune of a .194 average. Hernandez saved 32 of 33 opportunities, notched a 1.92 ERA in a league-leading 80 games, and went 9–3 for the world champion Tigers.

1984 AL WINNING STATS

WINS	9
LOSSES	3
PCT.	.750
ERA	1.92
GAMES	80
INNINGS	140.1
HITS	96
BASE ON BALLS	36
STRIKEOUTS	112
SAVES	32

1987 NL WINNING STATS

WINS	5
LOSSES	3
PCT.	.625
ERA	2.83
GAMES	65
INNINGS	89
HITS	79
BASE ON BALLS	28
STRIKEOUTS	74
SAVES	40

MARK DAVIS—NL 1989

The big southpaw was a runaway winner with 44 saves and a 1.85 ERA. Davis held batters to a piddly .200 average and helped the Padres to a second-place finish in the AL West.

1989 NL WINNING STATS

WINS	4
LOSSES	3
PCT.	.571
ERA	1.85
GAMES	70
INNINGS	92.2
HITS	66
BASE ON BALLS	31
STRIKEOUTS	92
SAVES	44

DENNIS ECKERSLEY—AL 1992

The demonstrative "Eck" also earned MVP honors with incredible numbers: 51 saves in 54 chances, a 7–1 record, a paltry 1.91 ERA, and only 11 walks in 80 innings. However, in the fourth game of the World Series, Eckersley allowed Sandy Alomar to tie with a home run. The Blue Jays went on to win the game and ultimately defeat Oakland 4–2 in the Series.

1992 AL WINNING STATS

WINS	7
LOSSES	1
PCT.	.875
ERA	1.91
GAMES	69
INNINGS	80
HITS	62
BASE ON BALLS	11
STRIKEOUTS	93
SAVES	51

Woulda, Shoulda, Coulda

Pitchers Who Were Good Enough to Win the Cy Young Award—But Didn't

The main reason the Cy Young Award is so special is that more than one pitcher, in most years, is deserving of the award. Yet, only one pitcher will win it (except in the rare event of a tie). Some pitchers have never won the award, yet are either in the Hall of Fame or soon will be.

NOLAN RYAN

No pitcher has ever thrown in more seasons, had more no-hitters, or struck out more batters than Nolan Ryan has. And only eleven pitchers have ever won more games. Yet he never won a Cy Young Award.

How could that be?

Simple. Ryan was never deemed to have had a better season than all other pitchers during any one season.

That is the nature of such awards—for every deserving winner, there are deserving runners-up who just weren't as good that year, no matter how outstanding their career statistics are.

Indeed, few Cy Young Award winners will ever match Ryan's career stats: 27 seasons and 5,714 strikeouts, both major league records, and 324 wins, which ties him with Don Sutton for twelfth place. But for one season, Nolan was never the best pitcher in his league—or so the voters thought.

But what about his 1981 season? It could be argued that Ryan, then pitching for the Houston Astros, was the best pitcher in the National League. In that season, he twirled his fifth no-hitter, breaking the career tie he had shared with Sandy Koufax. He also held batters to a meager .188 average and recorded a microscopic 1.69 earned run average, both league-leading marks in that strike-shortened season. He also won 11 games, yet he finished a distant fourth in the vot-

ing behind rookie sensation Fernando Valenzuela, who won 13 games. In the voting, Valenzuela narrowly edged out Cy Young perennials Tom Seaver and Steve Carlton.

Or perhaps Ryan should have won the award for his 1973 season in the American League with the California Angels, in which he threw 2 of his career 7 no-hitters and struck out an astonishing 383 batters, still the major league mark. But when it came to Cy Young votes, he finished second, 88–62, to Jim Palmer, who won the first of his three Cy Young Awards.

For all the pluses of his spectacular career, there always seemed to be a negative factor or two that left Ryan a little short in the voting. For example, in 1973, when he won 21 games, had a 2.87 ERA, and held opponents to a .203 average, Ryan also lost 16 games and walked a hefty 162 batters. That year Palmer was 22–9 with a league-leading 2.40 ERA.

The perception that Ryan was a wild, near-.500 pitcher continued the following year when he won 22 games, just 3 fewer than Cy Young winner Catfish Hunter of the Oakland A's. Despite striking out 367 batters and allowing a league-low .190 batting average and only 6 hits per game, Ryan finished third in the voting. Again, 16 losses and a staggering 202 walks worked against the flamethrower.

So what does a guy have to do to win a Cy Young Award?

Ryan probably asked himself that question more than once during his marvelous career. One thing is for certain: he wasn't the only pitcher ever to ask the question. There are many pitchers—some great over a career, some great for a season—who pitched well enough to win a Cy Young Award but were beaten in the voting by someone who was just a little better.

1973 NL STATS	
WINS	21
LOSSES	16
PCT.	.568
ERA	2.87
GAMES	41
INNINGS	326
HITS	238
BASE ON BALLS	162
STRIKEOUTS	383
SHUTOUTS	4
1974 NL STATS	
WINS	22
LOSSES	16
PCT.	.579
ERA	2.89
GAMES	42
INNINGS	333
HITS	221
BASE ON BALLS	202
STRIKEOUTS	367
SHUTOUTS	3
1981 NL STATS	
WINS	11
LOSSES	5
PCT.	.688
ERA	1.69
GAMES	21
INNINGS	149
HITS	99
BASE ON BALLS	68
STRIKEOUTS	140
SHUTOUTS	3

Nolan Ryan, owner of the fastest fastball, was never able to obtain a Cy Young Award. He is shown here on the mound for the Houston Astros.

BERT BLYLEVEN

This Dutch native threw more than 4,800 innings, ranks third on the all-time strikeout list with 3,701, amassed 60 shutouts, and compiled a total of 279 career wins. In 1984 he went 19–7 with a 2.87 ERA on a Cleveland team that won only 75 games. Blyleven, however, finished third in the balloting behind two relievers, Willie Hernandez of the Detroit Tigers (who was also named the league's Most Valuable Player) and Dan Quisenberry of the Kansas City Royals (who had a league-leading 44 saves).

JIM BUNNING

Bunning was only the second major league pitcher—after Cy Young himself—to win at least 100 games in each league. He pitched for the AL Detroit Tigers for nine years and in the National League for eight more, six of those with the Philadelphia Phillies. He led the American League with 20 wins in 1957, but was completely ignored by the Cy Young voters, who that year overwhelmingly chose 21-game winner Warren Spahn of the Milwaukee Braves.

Bunning had four 19-win seasons, including one in 1964 when he led the National League by walking just 1.5 batters per game for the Phillies. He also pitched a perfect game that year against the New York Mets in Shea Stadium.

ELROY FACE

In 1959, this premier forkballer won his first 17 decisions and finished with an 18–1 record in 57 relief appearances for the Pittsburgh Pirates. Face did not receive a single Cy Young vote, despite a league-leading .947 winning percentage, 10 saves, and a 2.70 ERA in 93 innings of relief.

1984 NL STATS

WINS	19
LOSSES	7
PCT.	.731
ERA	2.87
GAMES	33
INNINGS	245
HITS	204
BASE ON BALLS	74
STRIKEOUTS	170
SHUTOUTS	4

1957 NL STATS

WINS	20
LOSSES	8
PCT.	.714
ERA	2.69
GAMES	45
INNINGS	267.1
HITS	214
BASE ON BALLS	72
STRIKEOUTS	182
SHUTOUTS	1

1959 NL STATS

WINS	18
LOSSES	1
PCT.	.947
ERA	2.70
GAMES	57
INNINGS	93.1
HITS	91
BASE ON BALLS	25
STRIKEOUTS	69
SAVES	10

MARK FIDRYCH

"The Bird" was often in a world of his own, observing strange rituals that included talking to baseballs. In the end, though, the unorthodox Detroit Tigers hurler had AL hitters talking to themselves. In 1976 Fidrych was a runaway Rookie of the Year winner and runner-up to Jim Palmer in Cy Young voting, 108–51.

The Bird won 19 games and led the league with a 2.34 ERA and 24 complete games. He held hitters to a .235 average, but struck out only ninety-seven batters in 250 innings, while Palmer led the league with 22 wins and 159 strikeouts, and was fifth with a 2.51 ERA.

1976 NL STATS	
WINS	19
LOSSES	9
PCT.	.679
ERA	2.34
GAMES	31
INNINGS	250
HITS	217
BASE ON BALLS	53
STRIKEOUTS	97
SHUTOUTS	4

The BBWAA

The Baseball Writers' Association of America (BBWAA) was formed in 1908 to help better the working conditions of the scribes who covered the games. To be a member, a writer must work for a daily newspaper and cover a major league baseball team. The BBWAA hands out annual awards for Most Valuable Player, Cy Young winner, Rookie of the Year, and Manager of the Year, as voted on by two writers per team from each major league city.

Voters may vote on more than one award each year, but nobody gets to vote for both the Cy Young Award and the Most Valuable Player in the same year.

According to Jack Lang, the assistant secretary of the BBWAA, "That's so there's no trading off of votes." If this restriction didn't exist, a voter could, for instance, give his Cy Young vote to a pitcher to whom he might otherwise want to award the MVP, thus freeing up his MVP vote for a favored position player. Now in semiretirement, Lang served as the BBWAA's secretary-treasurer for thirty years and was succeeded in 1994 by Jack O'Connell.

The organization has about eight hundred active members and another 250 retired members. While working conditions have improved immeasurably over the years, Lang said writers sometimes get confronted by angry athletes and have to "roll with the punches."

In 1962, when Lang was covering the expansion New York Mets in their inaugural season, Lang had to take his own advice literally. On one occasion, slugging left fielder Frank Thomas, who hit 34 home runs in 1962 to go with his .266 batting average, once threw a punch at Lang's face.

"He grazed me on the neck," Lang recalled recently, "and I said, 'You fouled off another one.'" Thinking on one's feet isn't a specific requirement for membership in the BBWAA, but apparently it helps.

JERRY KOOSMAN

In 1976, Koosman finally emerged from the shadow of his New York Mets Hall of Fame teammate Tom Seaver. The smooth lefty went 21–10 with a 2.70 ERA while holding batters to a .226 average in his best Cy Young bid. But he finished second to the San Diego Padres' Randy Jones, who went 22–14 with a 2.74 ERA. Jones, who led the league with 25 complete games and 315 innings pitched, out-polled Koosman 96 to 69½.

1976 NL STATS	
WINS	21
LOSSES	10
PCT.	.677
ERA	2.70
GAMES	34
INNINGS	247
HITS	205
BASE ON BALLS	66
STRIKEOUTS	200
SHUTOUTS	3

MICKEY LOLICH

The portly Detroit lefty led the league in 1971 with 25 wins, 29 complete games, an incredible 376 innings, and an outstanding 308 strikeouts. He also had a solid 2.92 ERA and limited batters to a .237 average. But that year Vida Blue was right behind Lolich with 24 wins and 301 Ks, and out-did the Tigers star with a puny 1.82 ERA, a .189 opponents' batting average, and 8 losses (to Mickey's 14). It was a close vote, but Blue prevailed, 98–85. The next year, Lolich won 22 games, but finished third behind two-time winner Gaylord Perry and runner-up Wilbur Wood.

1971 NL STATS

WINS	25
LOSSES	14
PCT.	.641
ERA	2.92
GAMES	45
INNINGS	376
HITS	336
BASE ON BALLS	92
STRIKEOUTS	308
SHUTOUTS	4

JUAN MARICHAL

Probably the most deserving non-winner of all time, even more so than Nolan Ryan, Marichal had great control as well as a bulging grab bag of pitches and deliveries. In sixteen major league seasons, fourteen with the San Francisco Giants, "Manito" walked an average of just 1.8 batters per game, and led the league four times in that category. The Hall of Famer with 243 wins was a six-time 20-game winner, including 25 in both 1963 and 1966 and a career-high 26 in 1968. Yet nary a Cy Young Award.

What a tremendous year Marichal had in 1966. He went 25–6 for a league-leading .806 winning percentage, and also led the league in four other categories: fewest hits allowed per game, fewest walks per game, lowest batting average allowed, and lowest on-base percentage allowed. But Juan was aced out by the great Sandy Koufax, who won his third unanimous title. Sandy struck out ninety-five more batters than did Juan, won 27 games, and had the lowest ERA in the league for a record fifth straight year—1.73 to Marichal's 2.23.

In 1968 Marichal's league-leading 26 wins and 30 complete games were overshadowed by Bob Gibson's 1.12 ERA, 13 shutouts, and 22 wins. The next year, Juan led the league with a 2.10 ERA, 21 wins, and 205 strikeouts, but three-time Cy Young winner Tom Seaver won 25 games, had a 2.21 ERA, and struck out 208 while leading the New York Mets to history's most improbable world title.

1966 NL STATS	
WINS	25
LOSSES	6
PCT.	.806
ERA	2.23
GAMES	37
INNINGS	307.1
HITS	228
BASE ON BALLS	36
STRIKEOUTS	222
SHUTOUTS	4

SAM MCDOWELL

"Sudden Sam," a six-foot-five-inch lefty, had a great fastball that exploded into the strike zone. He averaged 8.9 strikeouts every 9 innings over his entire fifteen-year career. He was the top strikeout man in the American League five times while hurling for the Cleveland Indians.

In 1965, still the era of the single Cy Young winner, McDowell won 17 games and led the league with 325 strikeouts and a 2.18 ERA. But he was outdone by Sandy Koufax's 26 wins and then–major league record 382 strikeouts. In 1970, McDowell won 20, struck out a league-leading 304, and had a solid 2.92 ERA, fifth-best in the league. But three pitchers—Jim Perry, Dave McNally, and Mike Cuellar—each won 24 games. McDowell finished a close third in the voting with forty-five points, behind Perry's fifty-five and McNally's forty-seven.

1965 NL STATS

WINS	17
LOSSES	11
PCT.	.607
ERA	2.18
GAMES	42
INNINGS	273
HITS	178
BASE ON BALLS	132
STRIKEOUTS	325
SHUTOUTS	3

JACK MORRIS

From 1979 to 1988, Morris won 173 games for the Detroit Tigers and added 3 postseason wins during the team's 1984 world championship season. Morris forever solidified his reputation as a money pitcher in the 1991 World Series when he was a member of the world champion Minnesota Twins and threw a 10-inning shutout in Game Seven to beat the Atlanta Braves, 1–0.

But a hefty ERA in most of his seasons kept Morris from serious Cy Young consideration. His best ERA over that ten-year span was a not-too-slim 3.05, and that was in the strike-shortened 1981 season, when he led the league with 14 wins. But that year Cy Young winner Rollie Fingers saved 28 games, tallied a 1.04 ERA, and was named the American League's MVP. Most recently with the Toronto Blue Jays in 1992, Morris went 21–6, but held a 4.04 ERA.

1981 NL STATS

WINS	14
LOSSES	7
PCT.	.667
ERA	3.05
GAMES	25
INNINGS	198
HITS	153
BASE ON BALLS	78
STRIKEOUTS	97
SHUTOUTS	1

Woulda, Shoulda, Coulda
PHIL NIEKRO

This ancient knuckleballer pitched 5,404 innings over twenty-four seasons, the first twenty with the Atlanta Braves, eventually finishing right behind Nolan Ryan and Don Sutton with 318 career wins. Neikro was a three-time 20-game winner, including a 21–20 record in 1979, the same year his younger brother Joe went 21–11.

Phil led the league four times in both complete games and innings in the same season. In 1974, he went 20–13, leading the league in wins, throwing 6 shutouts, and totaling a 2.38 ERA. But Dodgers reliever Mike Marshall, with his 15 wins, 21 saves, and 2.42 ERA, took home the Cy Young Award that year.

1974 NL STATS	
WINS	20
LOSSES	13
PCT.	.606
ERA	2.38
GAMES	41
INNINGS	302
HITS	249
BASE ON BALLS	88
STRIKEOUTS	195
SHUTOUTS	6

DAN QUISENBERRY

"Quiz" led the league in saves five times, including a then-record 45 in 1983, the year LaMarr Hoyt of the Chicago White Sox won 24 games and the Cy Young Award. In 1984, Quisenberry saved 44 games, but finished second in the voting to another reliever, Willie Hernandez of the Detroit Tigers, who was also named the American League's MVP that season.

1983 NL STATS	
WINS	5
LOSSES	3
PCT.	.625
ERA	1.94
GAMES	69
INNINGS	139
HITS	118
BASE ON BALLS	11
STRIKEOUTS	48
SAVES	45

ROBIN ROBERTS

Had the Cy Young Award been established in 1952, when the Hall of Fame right-hander went 28–7 with a 2.59 ERA, Roberts might have been deemed a winner. That year he walked a paltry forty-five batters in a league-leading 330 innings. Roberts won 286 games in his career, including 20 or more in six straight seasons. The last year in that streak, however, came in 1955—just one year prior to the institution of the Cy Young Memorial Award.

1952 NL STATS	
WINS	28
LOSSES	7
PCT.	.800
ERA	2.59
GAMES	39
INNINGS	330
HITS	292
BASE ON BALLS	45
STRIKEOUTS	148
SHUTOUTS	3

JACK SANFORD

Sanford helped pitch the San Francisco Giants into the 1962 World Series with a 24–7 record, but his 3.43 ERA couldn't compete with Dodger Don Drysdale's 25 wins, 2.84 ERA, and league-leading 232 strikeouts.

1962 NL STATS	
WINS	24
LOSSES	7
PCT.	.774
ERA	3.43
GAMES	39
INNINGS	265.1
HITS	233
BASE ON BALLS	92
STRIKEOUTS	147
SHUTOUTS	2

DAVE STEWART

Oakland A Dave Stewart, the 1989 World Series MVP, won 20 or more games four years in a row but never won enough Cy Young votes to earn him the prized pitching honor. In 1987, Stewart tied Roger Clemens for the league lead with 20 wins, but also lost 13 games and had a hefty 3.68 ERA. Clemens won the award, losing only 9 while posting a 2.97 ERA.

In 1990, throwing for Oakland, "Stew" pitched 267 innings and went 22–11 with a 2.56 ERA, but lost in the voting to teammate Bob Welch, who posted a great 27–6 record with a 2.95 ERA.

1987 NL STATS	
WINS	20
LOSSES	13
PCT.	.606
ERA	3.68
GAMES	37
INNINGS	261.1
HITS	224
BASE ON BALLS	105
STRIKEOUTS	205
SHUTOUTS	1

DON SUTTON

Like Nolan Ryan, Sutton is further evidence that awesome career numbers don't ensure a Cy Young Award season. The smooth righty won 324 games and struck out 3,574, placing him fifth on the all-time K list.

In 1972, while pitching for the Los Angeles Dodgers, Sutton led the National League with 9 shutouts and allowed a league-low .189 batting average. He also won 19 games, struck out 207 batters, and had a 2.08 ERA, but had the misfortune of pitching in the same league as Steve Carlton, who won 27 games that year and earned a unanimous Cy Young vote.

In his only 20-win season, Sutton went 21–10 in 1976 with a 3.06 ERA, but was outpolled by winner Randy Jones (who won 22) and runner-up Jerry Koosman (who had 21 wins and a 2.70 ERA).

1972 NL STATS

WINS	19
LOSSES	9
PCT.	.679
ERA	2.08
GAMES	33
INNINGS	272.2
HITS	186
BASE ON BALLS	63
STRIKEOUTS	207
SHUTOUTS	9

FRANK TANANA

A 19-game winner in 1976 for the California Angels, the smoking lefty struck out 261 batters—second-best in the league—and held hitters to a .203 average. His 2.44 ERA ranked third in the league. Nevertheless, Tanana finished a distant third in the Cy Young balloting behind winner Jim Palmer and runner-up Mark Fidrych.

1976 NL STATS	
WINS	19
LOSSES	10
PCT.	.655
ERA	2.44
GAMES	34
INNINGS	288
HITS	212
BASE ON BALLS	73
STRIKEOUTS	261
SHUTOUTS	2

JOHN TUDOR

This crafty left-hander helped pitch the St. Louis Cardinals to the Eastern Division title in 1985 with one of the best seasons of the decade. Tudor (opposite, left) led the National League with 10 shutouts, won 21 games, and had an outstanding 1.93 ERA, but his pitching performance was eclipsed by Doc Gooden's monster year.

1985 NL STATS	
WINS	21
LOSSES	8
PCT.	.724
ERA	1.93
GAMES	36
INNINGS	275
HITS	209
BASE ON BALLS	49
STRIKEOUTS	169
SHUTOUTS	10

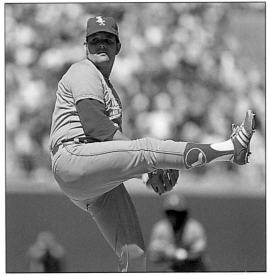

WILBUR WOOD

Over a four-year span, this knuckleballer won 20 or more games and pitched 300-plus innings for the White Sox in each of those years. In 1971, he went 22–13 and finished third in the voting behind winner Vida Blue and runner-up Mickey Lolich. In 1972, Wood (above) was 24–17 and was narrowly beaten out by Gaylord Perry in the Cy Young voting, 64–58.

1972 NL STATS	
WINS	24
LOSSES	17
PCT.	.585
ERA	2.51
GAMES	49
INNINGS	376.2
HITS	325
BASE ON BALLS	74
STRIKEOUTS	193
SHUTOUTS	8

1972

Bibliography

Aaseng, Nathan. *Steve Carlton, Baseball's Silent Strongman*. Minneapolis: Lerner Publications Co., 1984.

Eads Ward, Martha. *Steve Carlton, Star Southpaw*. New York: G.P. Putnam's Sons, 1975.

Gammons, Peter. *Rocket Man: The Roger Clemens Story*. New York: Viking Penguin, 1987.

Grabowski, John. *Sandy Koufax*. New York: James Charlton Associates, 1992.

Hoffman, Mark S., ed. *The World Almanac and Book of Facts*. New York: World Almanac, 1993.

James, Bill. *The Bill James Player Ratings Book*. New York: Collier Books, 1993.

Mayer, Ronald A. *Perfect! 14 Pitchers of Perfect Games*. Jefferson, N.C.: McFarland & Company, 1991.

McCarver, Tim. *Oh, Baby, I Love It!* New York: Villard Books, 1987.

McLain, Denny, with Mike Nahrstedt. *Strikeout: The Story of Denny McLain*. St. Louis: The Sporting News Publishing Co., 1988.

Mead, William B. *Two Spectacular Seasons*. New York: Macmillan Publishing, 1990.

Ritter, Lawrence, and Donald Honig. *The Image of Their Greatness*. New York: Crown Publishers, 1984.

Ryan, Nolan, with Jerry Jenkins. *Miracle Man: Nolan Ryan, The Autobiography*. Dallas: Word Publishing, 1992.

Shatzkin, Mike, and Jim Charlton. *The Ballplayers*. New York: Arbor House, 1990.

Thorn, John, and Pete Palmer. *Total Baseball*. New York: Warner Books, 1989.

Wolff, Rick, ed. *The Baseball Encyclopedia*, 9th ed. New York: MacMillan Publishing, 1993.

Index

Index

Photography Credits